Existential Psychology

D0060980

*Studies in
Psychology*

Existential Psychology

Edited by Rollo May

**William Alanson White Institute
of Psychoanalysis, Psychiatry, and Psychology**

SECOND EDITION

McGraw-Hill, Inc.
New York   St. Louis   San Francisco   Auckland
Bogotá   Caracas   Lisbon   London   Madrid
Mexico   Milan   Montreal   New Delhi   Paris
San Juan   Singapore   Sydney   Tokyo   Toronto

EXISTENTIAL PSYCHOLOGY

Second Edition

17 18 19 20 FGRFGR 9 8 7 6 5 4

Library of Congress Catalog Card Number: 70-79689

Manufactured in the United States of America

"For each thinker, the ultimate authority must be his own vision, through his own encounter with the reality at work in the facts—and he must find it there!"

William Ernest Hocking

"The ideal of science remains what it was in the time of Laplace: to replace all human knowledge by a complete knowledge of atoms in motion. . . . This is the heart of the matter. This is the origin of the whole scientific obscurantism under which we are suffering today. This is why we corrupt the conception of man, reducing him to an insentient automaton or to a bundle of appetites. This is why science denies us the possibility of acknowledging personal responsibility. This is why science can be invoked in support of totalitarian violence. Why science has become, as I have said before, the greatest source of dangerous fallacies today. . . .

"The question is: Can we get rid of all this terrible nonsense without jettisoning the beneficial guidance which science still offers us in other respects? I think this is extremely difficult. . . . But this will not remain so. The time will come when these scattered efforts will coalesce to a coherent movement of thought and then it will make rapid progress. . . ."

Michael Polanyi

Foreword to the Second Edition

The field of existential psychology has developed vastly during the eight years since the first version of this book was published. How great this change is can be seen from the fact that in the earlier edition it was possible to include 185 items; a nearly exhaustive listing of the writings in English, as our biographer Joseph Lyons indicates, "in which phenomenological or existentialist conceptions are applied explicitly to issues in the field of psychology." To do so today it would require close to 1,000 entries.

The vocabulary of existential psychology has entered firmly into our language; "existential crisis" is a common term now for the critical point in psychotherapy. Existential psychology is no longer a "foreign" school, but an attitude which permeates almost all brands of therapy in America. It has decisively influenced the present trend toward active therapy, "reality" therapy, and other forms of therapy that have emerged as correctives to orthodox psychoanalysis. And it has done this without becoming a separate school in itself. Most firmly of all, it is allied to the new "Third Force" psychology, so that most initiates in the field speak of "existential-humanistic" psychology, the two words hyphenated.

But the underlying concepts and forms of existential psychology have remained solid and perdurable while the surface has changed. The grounding in the lasting truths of the nature of man has stood this approach in good stead, which accounts for the fact that the basic writings of Heidegger and Sartre, Binswanger and Straus, are as important as ever.

In this revised edition, I have largely rewritten Chapter I. More has been inserted about William James, for example, whose existential groundwork has become more clear during the past eight years. I have also added a section on such new existential therapists as Laing and Ramirez, as well as a discussion of the expected criticisms of this approach to psychology.

Again, we have not tried to present a well worked out system, but to preserve the spontaneous character of the original papers by Allport, Feifel, Maslow, Rogers and my own case study in Chapter IV. We believe this book will be useful for the student who wishes to get a first-hand acquaintanceship with what existential psychology is.

Rollo May
February, 1969

Foreword to the First Edition

Although the existential approach has been most prominent in European psychology and psychiatry for two decades, it was practically unknown in this country until two years ago. Since then, some of us have been concerned that it may become *too* popular in some quarters, particularly in national magazines. But we have been comforted by a saying of Nietzsche's, "The first adherents of a movement are no argument against it."

The papers that follow, with the exception of the bibliography and certain sections added to the first chapter, were presented in the Symposium on Existential Psychology at the Annual Convention of the American Psychological Association in Cincinnati in September, 1959. Some of these papers are impressionistic and are so meant to be. Maslow's chapter is refreshingly direct: What's in existential psychology for us? Feifel's paper illustrates how this approach opens up for psychological inquiry such significant areas as attitudes toward death, heretofore conspicuous by their absence in psychology. My second chapter seeks to present a structural base in existential psychology for psychotherapy. Rogers' paper discusses, in particular, the relation of existential psychology to empirical research, and Allport's comments refer to some of the over-all implications of our inquiries.

Our purpose is not to give a systematic or definitive account of existential psychology—that cannot be done as yet. And so far as it can be, it has been done in the first three chapters of the volume *Existence* (33).* Our hope is that this book may serve as a stimulus to students who are interested in the field and that it may suggest topics and questions to be pursued. We trust that the bibliography will be an aid to students who may wish to read further about the many problems in the field.

Rollo May
1961

* Throughout the text, references in parentheses refer to the bibliography at the end of the volume.

Contents

I

The emergence of existential psychology

ROLLO MAY

In this introductory essay, I shall begin existentially by telling how this approach first impressed me. Then I shall discuss its emergence on the American scene with particular reference to William James. After some endeavors at defining my terms, I shall cite some questions that many of us have been asking in psychology for some years—questions which I believe call for an existential approach. I shall then present some of the newer forms of existential therapy, particularly in the work of Ephren Ramirez and Ronald Laing. Finally, I shall consider some of the criticisms of this approach, adding my own view of the difficulties and problems that existential psychology confronts today.

1

Some years ago, while working on my book *The Meaning of Anxiety*, I contracted tuberculosis and spent a year and a half lying in bed in a sanatorium. At this time there were no drugs for the disease; and, as I waited hour after hour and day after day until the end of each month to see whether the X-ray would show my cavity getting smaller or larger, I had plenty of time to ponder the meaning of anxiety—and plenty of first-hand data in myself and my fellow patients.

In the course of this illness, I studied the only two books written at that time on anxiety: *The Problem of Anxiety* by Freud and *The Concept of Dread* by Kierkegaard. I valued Freud's formulations—his first theory, that anxiety is the reemergence of repressed libido, and his second, that anxiety is the ego's reaction to the threat of the loss of the loved object. Kierkegaard, on the other hand, described anxiety as the struggle of the living being against nonbeing—which I was immediately experiencing in my struggle with death or the prospect of being a life-long invalid. He went on to point out that the real terror in anxiety is not this death as such, but the fact that each of us within himself is on both sides of the fight, that "anxiety is a desire for what one dreads, a sympathetic antipathy," as he put it. Thus, like an "alien power which lays hold of an individual, and yet one cannot tear one's self away, nor has a will to do so; for one fears, but what one fears one desires. Anxiety then makes the individual impotent." [1]

What struck me powerfully was that Kierkegaard was writing about *exactly what my fellow patients and I were going through*. Freud was not; he was writing on a different level, giving formulations of the psychic mechanisms by which anxiety comes about. Kierkegaard was portraying what is immediately experienced by human beings in crisis

---

[1] From Introduction to *Concept of Dread*; p. xii; quoted from his *Journal* (III A 233; Dru No. 402).

—specifically, the crisis of life against death, which was completely real to us patients. Kierkegaard was writing about a crisis that I believe is not in its essential form different from the various crises of people who come for therapy, or the crises that all of us experience in much more minute form a dozen times a day, even though we push the ultimate prospect of death far from our minds. Freud was writing on the technical level, where his genius was supreme; perhaps more than any man up to his time he knew *about* anxiety. Kierkegaard, a genius of a different order, was writing on the existential, ontological level; he *knew* anxiety.

This experience gave me, in a depth that goes far beyond mere theories or concepts and makes them seem absurdly superficial, an appreciation of what the existentialists have been trying to say. Camus' *The Plague,* Unamuno's *The Tragic View of Life,* Sartre's *The Flies,* Tillich's *The Courage to Be*—all these books were never again to be mere books to me. They are portrayals of contemporary man's struggle with a world that is marked by a dislocation as basic as my struggle with tuberculosis.

Kierkegaard and Freud do not represent a value dichotomy; both approaches are obviously necessary. Our real problem, rather, is given us by our cultural-historical situation. We in the Western world are the heirs of four centuries of technical achievement in power over nature and now over ourselves; this is our greatness and, at the same time, it is also our greatest peril. We are not in danger of denying the technical emphasis (of which Freud's tremendous popularity in this country was proof, if any proof were necessary). But rather we repress the opposite, the *awareness of being,* or the *ontological sense,* if I may use terms that I shall be discussing and defining more fully later. One consequence of this repression of the sense of being is that modern man's image of himself and his experience and concept of himself as a responsible individual have likewise disintegrated.

I make no apologies in admitting that I take very seriously the dehumanizing dangers in our tendency in modern science to make man over into the image of the machine, into the image of the techniques by which we study him. This tendency is not the fault of any "dangerous" men or "vicious" schools; it is rather a crisis brought upon us by our particular historical predicament. Karl Jaspers, both psychiatrist and existentialist philosopher, holds that we are actually in process of losing self-consciousness and that we may well be the last age of historical man. William Whyte, in his *Organization Man*, cautions that modern man's enemies may turn out to be a "mild-looking group of therapists, who . . . would be doing what they did to help you." He refers here to the tendency to use the social sciences in support of the social ethic of one's historical period; and thus the process of helping people may actually make them conform and tend toward the destruction of individuality. We cannot brush aside as unintelligent or antiscientific the cautions of such men; to try to do so would make *us* the obscurantists. There is a real possibility that we may be helping the individual adjust and be happy at the price of loss of his being.

The existentialist issue reaches to the roots of man's life and challenges him there. This partly accounts for both the negative and positive reactions to existential psychology and the fact that every group is either for or against the issue—but never neutral. This is why the persons most apt to be affected by this development, such as William James, whom we shall consider below, are those that experience some deep issue in their personal lives.

2

We immediately notice a curious paradox when we look at existentialism and the American scene. Whereas there is a great deal of latent hostility and outright resistance in this country toward existential psychology, there is at the same time a deep underlying affinity between this approach and our American character and thought. This is true in psychology as well as in other areas.

I shall cite here, for our demonstration, William James, who remains our greatest and most typical American psychologist and philosopher. "He was what we would now call an existentialist," Jacques Barzun states baldly in his review of a recent biography of James.[2] And, if I may relate his experience to my own, he became this not by theory but by hard experience. Burdened by melancholy, ill health, and depression—particularly in his twenties and thirties—James was often on the verge of suicide; he writes frequently of his yearning that someone could give him "a reason for wishing to live four hours longer." Specifically, it was this continual depression that caused James—all his life a man who had great difficulty deciding anything—to be so concerned with the problem of will. In his early thirties in Europe he "decided" one day that it was worth the wager to will to believe in freedom. He wrote then in his diary, "My first act of free will is to believe in free will." [3] Thus he acted on the belief that what matters is not that someone "give him a reason" but that he create meaning out of his life by an act of will. He was afterwards convinced—and as a therapist I find this judgment clinically sound—that his existential solution to the problem of will enabled him to deal with his depression. It is clear in his biography that at this point he began a tremendously fruitful and zestful life despite continual depressions and illnesses. Thus he could write, near the end of his chapter on will in *Principles of Psychology*:

"The huge world that girdles us about puts all sorts of questions to us, and tests us in all sorts of ways. . . . But the

[2] Gay Wilson Allen, *The Life and Work of William James* (Viking Press, 1967). Allen also identifies James as an existentialist: see pp. 138 and 167.

[3] *Ibid.*, p. 168.

deepest question that is ever asked admits of no reply but
the dumb turning of the will and tightening of our heart-
strings as we say, *"Yes, I will even have it so!"* . . . We answer by consents and non-consents and not by words. What
wonder that those dumb responses should seem our deepest
organs of communication with the nature of things! . . .
What wonder if the amount which we accord of it be the one
strictly underived and original contribution which we make
to the world!" [4]

One of the emphases James shared with the existentialists is that on *knowing by doing*. If I read to you a sentence,
"Truth exists for the individual only as he himself produces
it in action," you may well think I have picked up a book
by James. But you would be wrong: that was written, when
James was a toddler of two, by Sören Kierkegaard, the
father of modern existentialism; and the sentence echoes
down through American pragmatism. Both James and
Kierkegaard emphasized the *passionate immediacy of experience*.

As I have already indicated, James also believed with
Kierkegaard in the importance of *will*, arguing that you
can never know or discover truth by sitting in detachment
in an armchair. *Decision and commitment* are themselves
prerequisites to the discovery of truth. Like Nietzsche and
Schopenhauer before him, James did not believe epistemology was an exclusively cognitive function Conation is involved in every act of cognition. James' epistemology is
strikingly similar to that of Nietzsche in the *Will to Power*,
where Nietzsche holds that truth is the way a biological
group actualizes itself.

The friendly but heated disputes between James and his
friend Charles S. Peirce is a fascinating picture of the struggle between "existence and essence"—to introduce one of
the controversial phrases immediately. Several times Peirce
chided James for his existentialism, saying, "your existential

---

[4] William James, *Principles of Psychology*, Book II (New
York: Dover Publications), pp. 578–579.

universe is inexact," and, he went on, "you must have some invariable or exactly certain yardstick." [5] But James, undaunted as always in public, contended in his answering letter, "The real world is incongruent, indeterminant, and the logical terms only mark static *positions* in a flux which nowhere is static." The "exact relations form a splendid artificial scheme of tabulation, on which to catch whatever elements of the existential flux can be made to stick there." [6] Made to stick—yes, at the price of abstracting them from reality for purposes of logic and mathematics, which is laudable enough but also artificially stops the continuous flux.

At another place in his *Pragmatism* we find James answering both Peirce and his own father, whom he deeply loved but whose transcendental monism, related to Swedenborg and the Concord School of Philosophy, he could never stomach. Writing of man's actions, William James proclaims, "Does our act then create the world's salvation so far as it makes room for itself, so fast as it leaps into the gap? . . . Here I take the bull by the horns, and in spite of the whole crew of rationalists and monists, of whatever brand they may be, I ask *why not?*" [7]

This and the statement I quoted above make a curious forerunner of the later more extreme statement by Jean Paul Sartre: "existence precedes essence." [8] This is not the only side to James, however. He is credited by historians of science with being the beginner of American empiricism in psychology. Existence also requires essence James knew. And essence—at least this side of heaven—requires that it be made real by the existential efforts of those of us who do exist. We live in a constant interaction between the two.

[5,6] Ralph Barton Perry, *The Thought and Character of William James,* Brief Edition (paperback), New York: Harper & Row, 1964.

[7] William James, *Pragmatism* (Cleveland: Meridian Books, 1955), p. 186.

[8] James, *Principles, op. cit.,* p. 576.

James' humanism and his great breadth as a human being, furthermore, enabled him to bring art, religion, and
ethics into his thought without sacrificing his scientific integrity. He was impressed by life's "vast blooming confusion," and was inveterately opposed to those who would
cut life down to the size of their own limited and narrow
viewpoints. He was—like any good existentialist—not antiscientific but believed that science was made for man rather
than man for science. After a sympathetic account of empiricism in science, James writes:

> Science, however, must be constantly reminded that her pur-
> poses are not the only purposes, and that the order of uni-
> form causation which she has use for, and is therefore right
> in postulating, may be enveloped in a wider order, on which
> she has no claims at all.[9]

But the position of James as an "early existentialist" turns
out to be not so surprising after all. For when he came back
from Europe in the 1870s, he was committed, like Kierkegaard three decades earlier, to an attack on the reigning
panrationalism of Hegel, which identified truth with abstract concepts. Paul Tillich has this to say about James in
his historical survey of existential philosophy:

> Like the American philosopher William James . . . the ex-
> istential philosophers are appealing from the conclusion of
> "rationalistic" thinking which equates Reality with the ob-
> ject of thought, with relations or "essences," to Reality as
> men experience it immediately in their actual living. They
> consequently take their place with all those who have re-
> garded man's immediate experience as revealing more com-
> pletely the nature and traits of Reality than man's cognitive
> experience.[10]

Tillich terms James a philosopher; but he is, of course, a
psychologist as well. The confluence of these two disciplines

[9] James, *Principles, op. cit.,* p. 576.
[10] Paul Tillich, "Existential Philosophy," 5, *Journal of Hist.
Ideas* (1944), 44–47.

indicates another aspect of the existential approach: it deals with psychological categories—"experience," "anxiety," "will," and so forth—but it is concerned with understanding these aspects of man's life on the deeper level of *ontological* reality. Thus it is an error to think of existential psychology as a resurrection of the old "philosophical psychology" of the nineteenth century. The existential approach is not a movement back to the armchair of speculation but an endeavor to understand man's behavior and experience in terms of the presuppositions that underlie them—presuppositions that underlie our science and our image of man. It is the endeavor to understand man as *experiencing*, as the one to *whom* the experiences happen.

Adrian van Kaam, in reviewing the work of the Dutch psychologist J. Linschoten, describes how William James' search for a new image of man as a broader basis for psychology led him directly into the center of the development of phenomenology. (Phenomenology, the first stage in the development of existential psychology, will be illustrated and defined later.) Van Kaam's summary is so pertinent to our topic that we quote it in detail.[11]

> One of the leading European existential phenomenologists, J. Linschoten, wrote a book, *On the Way Towards a Phenomenology*, with the subtitle, "The Psychology of William James." . . . In the introduction to this book, the diary of Husserl is quoted by Linschoten, where the father of European phenomenology admits the influence of the thought of this great American, James, on his own thinking.[12]

[11] Adrian van Kaam, "The impact of existential phenomenology on the psychological literature of western Europe," paper published in *Review of Existential Psychology and Psychiatry*, 1 (1), 1961, pp. 62–91.

[12] "Although I was able to read only a few things and too little of James' Psychology," wrote Husserl in his diary, "it brought some lightning flashes. I saw how a courageous and original man did not let himself be shackled by any tradition

The book demonstrates in a well documented way that the hidden intention of James' thinking has been realized in the breakthrough of the new existential cultural awareness. James was groping towards a vaguely felt new phase in the history of Western mankind. Rooted in the Victorian period, he expressed continuous dissatisfaction with its exclusively onesided way of "existing" [13] in the world. Linschoten concludes, in his final chapter, that James was on the road towards a phenomenological psychology before Buytendijk, Merleau-Ponty, and Straus, and was already ahead of them in his concern for the *integration of an objectifying psychology within the frame of a descriptive psychology.*

The lack of systematization in James' work is based on the insight that the unity of man and of the world are not dependent on "the one rational method" but on the unity of the prerational world, the one world of experience, the one original integral source of the diverging questions which make for different sciences and different psychologies. This original integral source of all ways of existing in the world is the body, the origin of experience of the world. This origin of experience has two aspects: that which is the source of the experience and that which is experienced itself. Therefore, one can choose one of two viewpoints: one can describe and analyze experience and body as the original modes of existing within the world as has been done by such men as Merleau-Ponty, Straus, and Buytendijk; or one can describe and analyze experience and body in the time-space coherence of the experienced "reality" as has been done by such men as Skinner, Hull, Spence. The first way

------

but endeavored effectively to hold on to and describe what he saw. This influence was not unimportant for me . . . ." Later on Husserl mentioned James as the only one who noticed the phenomenon called "horizon." These points are from the interesting book entitled *On the Way Toward a Phenomenological Psychology: The Psychology of William James,* by Linschoten, Amedeo Gorki (tr.), and published by Duquesne University Press of Pittsburgh, 1968.

[13] [Van Kaam uses "existing" here and elsewhere in its strict etymological sense of "standing out" toward something (*exsistere*), [meaning a way of relating to the world, Editor.]

leads to what has been called a *descriptive* psychology, the second one to an *explaining* psychology. As soon as one of them makes its viewpoint absolute, they are no longer able to communicate with one another. James has tried to preserve their complementary mutuality. This is possible only on the basis of a theory of man as an integral source of experience, a theory of his original mode of existing, a phenomenology of the experienced world, which phenomenology is implicit in James.

This indicates, I may remark parenthetically, why those of us interested in psycho*therapy* are more apt to be concerned with the existential approach than our colleagues involved in laboratory research or the construction of theory. For we have taken our stand, of necessity, with human beings who are immediately suffering, struggling, and experiencing conflicts in a myriad of protean forms. This immediate experience is our milieu, and it gives us the reason as well as the data for the research that we do hand in hand with therapy. We have to deal with patients whose anxiety and suffering will not be healed by theories no matter how brilliant, or by abstract laws no matter how comprehensive. In this sense, it can be argued that psychotherapists are the "hard-headed" realistic professionals rather than our colleagues in the laboratory. Through this immediate interaction in psychotherapy, we achieve a quality of information and understanding of human beings that we could not get in any other way. For no person will go through the painful process of disclosing the deepest levels of his conflicts, his dreads, and his yearnings—certainly not to another person and rarely even to himself—unless by this process he has some hope of overcoming his blocks and alleviating his suffering.

3

At this point we pause to define our terms. Existentialism involves centering upon the *existing* person and emphasizes the human being as he is *emerging, becoming*. The word "existence" comes from the Latin root *exsistere,* meaning literally "to stand out, emerge."

Traditionally in Western culture, *existence* has been set over against *essence,* the latter being the emphasis upon immutable principles, truth, logical laws, and so forth, that are assumed to stand above and beyond any given existence. In endeavoring to separate reality into its discrete parts and to formulate abstract laws for these parts, Western science has by and large been *essentialist* in character. Mathematics is the ultimate, pure form of this essentialist approach. One can have four unicorns as well as four apples; it makes absolutely no difference for mathematics whether the unicorns exist or not. In psychology, the endeavors to see human beings in terms of forces, drives, conditioned reflexes, and so on, illustrate the approach via essences. The emphasis on essences was dominant in Western thought—with such notable exceptions (to name only a few) as Socrates, Augustine, and Pascal—until roughly a hundred years ago. The peak was reached, the most systematic and comprehensive expression of "essentialism" became in Hegel's panrationalism an endeavor to encompass all reality in a system of concepts that identified reality with abstract thought. It was against Hegel that Kierkegaard, and later Nietzsche and James, revolted so strenuously. (The reader who wishes to follow this historical development in greater detail is referred to the first chapter of *Existence.*)[14] This wing in philosophy has emerged hand in hand with the new developments in science, particularly the physics of Bohr and Heisenberg.

Paul Tillich expresses our historical point well:

> In contrast to the situation in the last three years after the second World War, when most people identified existentialism with Sartre, it is now common knowledge in this

[14] *Existence: A New Dimension in Psychiatry and Psychology,* Rollo May, Ernest Angel, Henri Ellenberger, eds. (New York: Basic Books, 1958). Now published in paperback, Clarion Books, Simon and Schuster, 1967.

country that existentialism in the western intellectual history starts with Pascal in the 17th century, has an underground history in the 18th century, a revolutionary history in the 19th century, and an astonishing victory in the 20th century. Existentialism has become the style of our period in all realms of life. Even the analytic philosophers pay tribute to it by withdrawing into formal problems and leaving the field of material problems to the existentialists in art and literature.

There are, however, only rare moments in this monumental development in which almost pure existentialism has been reached. An example is Sartre's doctrine of man. I refer to a sentence in which the whole problem of essentialism and existentialism comes into the open, his famous statement that man's essence is his existence. ["Existence precedes essence."] The meaning of this sentence is that man is a being of whom no essence can be affirmed, for such an essence would introduce a permanent element, contradictory to man's power of transforming himself indefinitely. But if we ask whether this statement has not, against its intention, given an assertion about man's essential nature, we must say, certainly, it has. Man's particular nature is his power to create himself. And if the further question is raised of how such a power is possible and how it must be structured, we need a fully developed essentialist doctrine in order to answer; we must know about his body and his mind, and, in short, about those questions which for millennia have been discussed in essentialist terms.

I agree with Sartre when he emphasizes, "We *are* our choices," but I would add, "within the limits of our given world." We all are born of woman, struggle through stages of growth the best we can, and ultimately die; and what we think about it will not change these brute facts. It will, however, vastly change *how* we negotiate this threescore and ten. "Essences" must not be ruled out—they are presupposed in logic, mathematical forms, and other aspects of truth which are not dependent upon any individual's decision or whim. But that is not to say that we can adequately describe or understand a living human being, or any living organism, or an "essentialist" basis. *There is no such thing as truth or reality for a living human being except as he participates in it, is conscious of it, has some relationship to it.* We can demonstrate at every moment of the day in our psychotherapeutic work that only the truth that comes alive, becomes more than an abstract idea but is "felt on the pulse," only the truth that is genuinely experienced on all levels of being, including what is called subconscious and unconscious but never excluding the element of conscious decision and responsibility—only this truth has the power to change a human being.

The existentialist emphasis in psychology does not, therefore, deny the validity of conditioning, the formulation of drives, the study of discrete mechanisms, and so on. It only holds that we can never explain or understand any *living* human being on that basis. And the harm arises when the image of man is exclusively based on such methods. There seems to be the following "law" at work: the more accurately and comprehensively we can describe a given mechanism, the more we lose the existing person. *The more absolutely and completely we formulate the forces or drives, the more we are talking about abstractions and not the living human being.* For the living person (who is not hypnotized or drugged or in some other way placed in an artificial position, such as in a laboratory, in which his element of decision and his responsibility for his own existence are temporarily suspended for the purposes of the experiment) always transcends the given mechanism and always experiences the "drive" or "force" in his unique way. The distinction is whether the "person has meaning in terms of the mechanism" or the "mechanism has meaning in terms of the person." The existential emphasis is firmly on the latter.

True, the term "existentialist" was dubious and confused until recently, associated as it was with the beatnik movement at one extreme and with esoteric, untranslatable, Germanic, philosophical concepts at the other. True also, the movement collected the "lunatic fringe" groups—to which existential psychology and psychiatry are by no means immune. I used to ask myself whether the word had become so dubious as to be no longer useful. But the term "existential" does have important historical meanings that ought to be saved. Fortunately at this time the term has become part of our day-to-day vocabulary, standing for emphasis on the reality of the immediate experience in the present moment.

In psychology and psychiatry, the term demarcates an *attitude*, an approach to human beings, rather than a special school or group. It is doubtful whether it makes sense to speak of "*an* existential psychologist or psychotherapist" in contradistinction to other schools. Existentialism is not a system of therapy but an attitude toward therapy. Though it has led to many advances of technique, it is not a set of new techniques in itself but a concern with the understanding of the structure of the human being and his experience that must underlie all techniques. This is why it makes sense, if I may say so at the risk of being misunderstood, to say that every psychotherapist is existential to the extent that he is a good therapist. Almost all therapists—including some Freudians—claim that they are influenced by and exemplify existentialist principles.

4

One may agree with my sentiments here but hold that the existentialist approach, with such terms as "being" and "nonbeing," is not of much help. Some readers will already have concluded that their suspicion was only too correct, that this form of psychology is hopelessly vague and horribly muddled. Carl Rogers remarks in Chapter V of this book that many American psychologists must find these terms abhorrent because they sound so general, so philosophical, so untestable. Rogers goes on to point out, however, that he had no difficulty in putting the existential principles in therapy into empirically testable hypotheses.

I take the bull by the horns and argue that *without* some concepts of "being" and "nonbeing" we cannot even understand our most commonly used psychological mechanisms. Take, for example, *transference* and *repression*. The usual discussions of these terms, unconvincing and psychologically unreal, hang in midair precisely because we have lacked an underlying structure on which to base them. The concept of transference was one of Freud's great contributions, both in his own judgment and in that of many of the rest of us. There are vast implications for therapy in the phenomenon that the patient brings into the consulting room his previous or present relationships with father, mother, lover, child, and proceeds to perceive the therapist as he does those creatures and build his world with the therapist in the same way as he does with them.

But the concept of transference presents us with unending difficulties if we take it by itself, that is, without a norm of relationship that is grounded in the nature of man as such. It can be a handy and ever-useful defense, as Thomas Szasz puts it; the therapist can hide behind it to protect himself from the anxiety of direct encounter. Also the concept of transference can undermine the whole experience and sense of reality in therapy; the two persons in the consulting room become "shadows," and everyone else in the world does too. It can erode the patient's sense of responsibility and can rob the therapy of much of the dynamic for the patient's change. What has been lacking is a concept of encounter, within which, and only within which, transference has genuine meaning. *Transference is to be understood as the distortion of encounter.*

Encounter is one expression of being. I mean the word to refer to the fact that in the therapeutic hour a total relationship is going on between two people, which involves a number of different levels. One level is that of real persons: I am glad to see my patient (my response varying on different days and depending chiefly on the amount of sleep I have had the night before.) Our seeing each other allays the physical loneliness to which all human beings are heir. Another level is that of *friends;* we trust—for we have seen a lot of each other—that the other has some genuine concern for listening and understanding. A third level is felt as *erotic*—which needs to be accepted by the therapist if he is to listen understandingly and also if he is to avail himself of this dynamic resource for change.[15] A fourth level is that of *esteem*, the capacity which inheres in interpersonal relations for self-transcending concern for another's welfare. All of these constitute a real relationship, the distortion of which is transference.

The term "repression," for another example, obviously refers to a phenomenon we observe all the time, a dynamism that Freud clearly, and in many forms, described. The mechanism is generally explained by saying that the child represses into unconsciousness certain impulses, such as sex and hostility, because the culture, in the form of parental figures, disapproves; and the child must protect his own security from these persons. But this culture that assumedly disapproves is made up of the very same people who do the repressing. Is it not an allusion and much too simple, therefore, to speak of the culture over against the individual in such fashion and to make it our whipping boy? Furthermore, where did we get the idea that children or adults are so concerned with security and libidinal satisfactions? Are these not carryovers from our work with the *neurotic*, anxious child and the *neurotic* adult?

Certainly the neurotic, anxious child *is* compulsively concerned with security; and certainly the neurotic adult, and we who study him, read our later formulations back into the unsuspecting mind of the child. But is not the normal child just as truly interested in moving out into the world, exploring, following his curiosity and sense of adventure—going out "to learn to shiver and to shake," as the nursery rhyme puts it? And if we block these needs

[15] I use "erotic" here in the general sense in which all kinds of relationships and things have a sexual tone—movies, books, and so forth. Obviously it is not acted upon in therapy but kept as part of the transference.

of the child, do we not get a traumatic reaction from him just as we do when we take away his security? I, for one, believe we have overemphasized the human being's concern with security and survival satisfactions because they so neatly fit our cause-and-effect way of thinking. I believe Nietzsche was more accurate when he described man as *the organism who makes certain values—prestige, power, tenderness, love—more important than pleasure and even more important than survival itself.*[16]

The upshot of our argument here is that we can understand such a mechanism as repression only on the deeper

[16] This is the point Binswanger is making in the case of *Ellen West,* translated in the volume *Existence*. By means of the discussion of the psychological illness and suicide of Ellen West, he asks whether there are times when an existence, in order to fulfill itself, must destroy itself. In this case, Binswanger, like so many of his European psychiatric and psychological colleagues, discusses a case for the purpose of delving into the understanding of some problem about human beings rather than for the purpose of illustrating how the case should or should not be managed therapeutically. In presenting the case, we assumed, as editors of *Existence,* that it, like the other cases, would be understood on the basis of the purposes and assumptions of its author in writing it. Alas, this was an unrealistic assumption! The case is almost universally discussed—and from that point of view justly criticized—in this country from the point of view of what therapy should have been given Ellen West. But if it had been Binswanger's purpose to discuss techniques of therapy, he would not have taken a case from the archives of half a century ago in his sanatorium. He seeks, rather, to ask this most profound of all questions: Does the human being have needs and values that transcend its own survival, and are there not situations when the existence, in order to fulfill itself, needs to destroy itself? The implication of this question is in the most radical way to question simple adaptation, length of life, and survival as ultimate goals. It is similar to Nietzsche's point referred to above and also similar to Maslow's emphasis when he brings out that the self-actualizing personalities which he studied *resist* acculturation.

level of the meaning of the person's potentialities. In this respect, "being" is to be defined as the *individual's unique pattern of potentialities*. These potentialities will be partly shared with other individuals but will in every case form a unique pattern for this particular person.

We must ask the following questions, therefore, if we are to understand repression in a given person: What is this person's relation to his own potentialities? What goes on that he chooses, or is forced to choose, to block off from his awareness something that he knows and on another level *knows that he knows?* In my own work in psychotherapy, there appears more and more evidence that anxiety in our day arises not so much out of fear of lack of libidinal satisfactions or security but rather out of the patient's fear of his own powers and the conflicts that arise from that fear. This is the neurotic pattern of contemporary outer directed, organizational man and may well be the neurotic personality of our time.

The unconscious, then, is not to be thought of as a reservoir of impulses, thoughts, and wishes that are culturally unacceptable. I define it rather as *those potentialities for knowing and experiencing that the individual cannot or will not actualize*. On this level, we shall find that the simple mechanism of repression, which we blithely started with, is infinitely less simple than it looks; that it involves a complex struggle, as in my tuberculosis, of the individual's *being* against the possibility of *nonbeing;* that it cannot be adequately comprehended in "ego" and "not ego" terms, or even "self" and "not self"; and that it inescapably raises the question of the human being's freedom with respect to his own potentialities. This margin of freedom must be assumed if one is to deal with an existing person. In this margin resides the individual's responsibility for himself, which even the therapist cannot take away.

Thus every mechanism or dynamism, every force or drive, presupposes an underlying structure that is infinitely greater than the mechanism, drive, or force itself. And note that I do not say it is the sum total of the mechanisms. It is not the sum total, though it includes all the mechanisms, drives, or forces: it is the underlying structure from which they derive their meaning. This structure is, to use one definition proposed above, the *pattern of potentiality* of the living individual man *of whom* the mechanism is one expression. The given mechanism is one of a multitude of ways in which he actualizes his potentiality. Surely one can abstract a given mechanism like repression or regression for study and arrive at formulations of forces and drives that seem to be operative; but the study will have meaning only if one says at every point, "I am abstracting such and such a form of behavior." One also must make clear at every point *what* one is abstracting *from*, namely the living man who *has* these experiences, the man *to whom* these things happen.

5

In a similar vein, I have been struck, as a practicing therapist and teacher of therapists, by how often our concern with trying to understand the patient in terms of the mechanisms by which his behavior takes place blocks our understanding of what he really is experiencing. (An actual case is used in Chapter IV to illustrate this.)

If, as I sit with a patient, I am chiefly thinking of the *whys* and *hows* of the way the problem came about, I will have grasped everything *except the most important thing of all, the existing person*. Indeed, I will have grasped everything except the only real source of data I have, namely, this experiencing human being, this person now emerging, becoming, "building world," as the existential psychologists put it, immediately in this room with me.

This is where *phenomenology*, the first stage in the existential psychotherapeutic movement, has been a helpful breakthrough for many of us. Phenomenology is the endeavor to take the phenomena as given. It is the disciplined effort to clear one's mind of the presuppositions that so often cause us to see in the patient only our own theories or the dogmas of our own systems. It is the effort to experience instead the phenomena in their full reality as they present themselves. It requires the attitude of openness and readiness to hear—aspects of the art of listening in psychotherapy that are generally taken for granted and sound so easy but are actually exceedingly difficult.

Note that we say *experience* the phenomena, not merely *observe*. Harry Stack Sullivan uses the phrase "participant observer" to include this element of the therapist's participating in the world of the patient. We need to be able, as far as possible, to catch what the patient is communicating on many different levels, not only the words he utters but his facial expressions, his gestures, the distance from us at which he sits, various feelings that he will have and communicate subtly as messages even though he cannot verbalize them directly. There is always a great deal of subliminal communication on levels below what either the patient or therapist may be conscious of at the moment. This points toward a controversial area that is most difficult in the training and practice of therapists but that is unavoidable because it is so important, namely, empathetic and "telepathic" communication. I wish only to say this experiencing of the communications of the patient on many different levels at once is one aspect of what the existential psychiatrists like Binswanger call *presence*.

Phenomenology requires an "attitude of disciplined naivete," in Robert MacLeod's phrase. Commenting on this phrase, Albert Welleck adds his own, "an ability to *experience critically*." This brings us to a common misunderstanding of the existential approach—that it presupposes conceptless experience. It is not possible, in my judgment, to listen to any words or even to give our attention to anything without some assumed concepts, some constructs in our own mind by which we hear and orient ourselves in our world at that moment. But the radical difference is that in existentialism the concept is used as a tool for understanding rather than vice versa. The important terms "disciplined" in MacLeod's phrase and "critically" in Wellek's refer, I take it, to the difficult attainment of objectivity—that whereas we must have concepts as we listen, our aim in therapy is to make our own constructs sufficiently flexible so that we can listen in terms of the patient's constructs and hear in the patient's language.

Phenomenology has many complex ramifications, particularly as developed by Edmund Husserl, who decisively influenced not only the philosophers Heidegger and Sartre but also the psychiatrists Minkowski, Straus, and Binswanger, the psychologists Buytendijk, Merleau-Ponty, and many others. (The student may find a survey of psychological phenomenology in Ellenberger's chapter in *Existence* and may pursue it further in the references in the bibliography at the end of this book.)

Sometimes the phenomenological emphasis in psychotherapy is used as a rationalization for the disparagement of the learning of technique or as a reason for not studying the problems of diagnosis and clinical dynamics. I think this is an error. What is important, rather, is to apprehend the fact that the technical and diagnostic concerns are on a different level from the understanding that takes place in the immediate encounter in therapy. The mistake is in confusing them or letting one absorb the other. The student and practicing psychologist must steer his course between the Scylla of letting knowledge of techniques be a substitute for direct understanding and communication with the patient, and the Charybdis of assuming that he acts in a rarified atmosphere of clinical purity without any concepts at all.

Certainly it is true that students learning therapy often become preoccupied with techniques; this is the strongest anxiety-allaying mechanism available to them in the turmoil-fraught encounters in psychotherapy. Indeed, one of the strongest motivations for dogmatism and rigid formulations among psychotherapeutic and analytic schools of all sorts lies right here—the technical dogma protects the psychologist and psychiatrist from their own anxiety. But to that extent, the techniques also protect the psychologist or psychiatrist from understanding the patient; they block off the full presence in the encounter that is essential to understanding what is going on. One student in a case seminar on existential psychotherapy put it succinctly when he remarked that one of the things he had learned was that "understanding does not follow knowledge of dynamics."

There is, however, a danger of "wild eclecticism" in these phenomenological and existential approaches to therapy when they are used without the rigorous clinical study and thought that precedes any expertness. Knowledge of techniques and the rigorous study of dynamics in the training of the psychotherapist should be presupposed. Our situation is analogous to that of the artist: long and expert training is necessary; but if, at the moment of painting, the artist is preoccupied with technique or technical questions—a preoccupation every artist knows arises exactly at those points at which some anxiety overtakes him—he can be sure nothing creative will go on.

Diagnosis, for example, is a legitimate and necessary function, particularly at the beginning of therapy; but it is a function different from the therapy itself and requires a different attitude and orientation to the patient. There is something to be said for the attitude that once one gets into therapy with a patient and has decided on the general direction, one forgets for the time being the diagnostic question. (We shall later discuss Dr. Ramirez, who is very outspoken about this.) By the same token, questions of technique will arise in the therapist's mind from time to time as the therapy proceeds. One of the characteristics of existential psychotherapy is that the technique changes.

These changes will not be hit and miss, however, but will depend on the needs of the patient at given times.

If this discussion sounds unconcluded and gives the appearance of straddling the issue of "technique" on one side and "understanding" on the other, the appearance is indeed correct. The whole topic of the "technical-objective" versus the "understanding-subjective" attitude has been on a falsely dichotomized basis in our psychological and psychiatric discussions. There is a dialectical process that goes on, parallel to the dialectical process in all acts of consciousness. The problem needs to be restated on the basis of the concept of the existence of the patient as *being-in-the-world* and the therapist as existing in and participating in this world. I wish only to state my conviction here that such a reformulation is possible and gives promise of taking us out of our present dichotomy on this topic. And in the meantime, I wish as a practical expedient to take my stand against the nascent antirational tendencies in the existential approach. Though I believe that therapists are to a great extent born and not made, it inheres in one's integrity to be cognizant of the fact that there also is a great deal we can learn!

6

Another question that has perennially perplexed many of us in psychology has already been implied above, and we now turn to it explicitly. What are the presuppositions that underlie our science and our practice? I do not ask what is our "scientific method"; already a good deal of attention has been paid, and rightly, to the problem of methodology in science. But every method is based on certain presuppositions about the nature of man, the nature of his experience, and so forth. These presuppositions are partially conditioned by our culture and by the particular point in history at which we stand. As far as I can see, this crucial area is almost always sloughed over in psychology: we tend to assume uncritically and implicitly that our particular method is true for all time. The statement that science has built-in self-corrective measures—which is partially true—cannot be taken as a reason for overlooking the fact that our particular science is culturally and historically conditioned and is thereby limited even in its self-corrective measures.

At this point, the existential insistence is that *the psychologist must continually analyze and clarify his own presuppositions*. Our presuppositions always limit and constrict what we see in a problem, experiment, or therapeutic situation; there is no escape from this aspect of our human "finiteness." The naturalist perceives in man what fits his naturalistic spectacles; the positivist sees the aspects of experience that fit the logical forms of his propositions; and it is well known that different therapists of different schools will see in the same dream of a patient the dynamics that fit the theory of their particular school. The old parable of the blind men and the elephant is written large on the activities of men in the enlightened twentieth century as well as those of earlier, more "benighted" ages. Bertrand Russell puts the problem well with respect to physical science: "Physics is mathematical not because we know so much about the physical world but because we know so little; it is only its mathematical properties that we can discover."

No one—physicist, psychologist, or anyone else—can leap out of his historically conditioned skin. The one way we can keep the presuppositions underlying our particular method from unduly biasing our efforts is to know consciously what they are and so not to absolutize or dogmatize them. Thus we have at least a chance of refraining from forcing our subjects or patients upon our "Procrustean couches" and lopping off, or refusing to see, what does not fit.

In Ludwig Binswanger's little book *Sigmund Freud: Reminiscences of a Friendship*, which relates his conversations and correspondence with Freud, there are some interesting interchanges illustrating this point. The friendship between Freud, the psychoanalyst, and Binswanger, a leading existential psychiatrist of Switzerland, was lifelong and tender; and it marks the only instance of Freud's continuing in friendship with someone who differed radically with him.

Shortly before Freud's eightieth birthday, Binswanger wrote an essay describing how Freud's theory had radically deepened clinical psychiatry; but he added that Freud's own existence as a person pointed beyond the deterministic presuppositions of his theory.

> Now [with Freud's psychoanalytic contribution] man is no longer merely an animated organism, but a "living being" who has origins in the finite life process of this earth, and who dies its life and lives its death; illness is no longer an externally or internally caused disturbance of the "normal" course of a life on the way to its death.[17]

But Binswanger went on to point out that he believed that in Freud's theory man is not yet man in the full sense of the word:

> . . . for to be a man does not mean merely to be a creature begotten by living-dying life, cast into it and beaten about, and put in high spirits or low spirits by it; it means to be a being that looks its own and mankind's fate in the face, a being that is "steadfast," i.e., one taking its own stance, or one standing on its own feet. . . . The fact that our lives are determined by the forces of life, is only one side of the truth; the other is that we determine these forces as our fate. Only the two sides together can take in the full problem of sanity and insanity. Those who, like Freud, have forged their fates with the hammer—the work of art he has created in the medium of language is sufficient evidence of this—can dispute this fact least of all.[18]

[17] L. Binswanger, *Sigmund Freud: Reminiscences of a Friendship* (New York: Grune & Stratton, 1957), p. 90.
[18] *Ibid.*, 90.

Then, on the occasion of Freud's eightieth birthday, the Viennese Medical Society invited Binswanger, along with Thomas Mann, to deliver papers at the anniversary celebration. Freud himself did not attend, not being in good health and also, as he wrote Binswanger, not being fond of anniversary celebrations ("They seem to be too much on the American model."). Binswanger spent two days with Freud in Vienna at the time of this birthday and remarked that in these conversations he was again impressed by how far Freud's own largeness and depth of humanity as a man surpassed his scientific theories.

In his paper at the celebration, Binswanger gave credit to Freud for having enlarged and deepened our insight into human nature more, perhaps, than anyone since Aristotle. But he went on to point out that these insights wore "a theoretic-scientific garb that as a whole appeared to me too 'one-sided' and narrow." He held that Freud's great contribution was in the area of *homo natura,* man in relation to nature (*Umwelt*)—drives, instincts, and similar aspects of experience. And as a consequence, Binswanger believed that in Freud's theory there was only a shadowy, epiphenomenal understanding of man in relation to his fellowmen (*Mitwelt*) and that the area of man in relation to himself (*Eigenwelt*) was omitted entirely.

Binswanger sent a copy of the paper to Freud and a week later received a letter from him containing the following sentences:

> As I read it I was delighted with your beautiful language, your erudition, the vastness of your horizon, your tactfulness in contradicting me. As is well known, one can put up with vast quantities of praise. . . . *Naturally, for all that you have failed to convince me.*[19] I have always confined myself to the ground floor and basement of the edifice. You maintain that by changing one's point of view, one can also see the upper story, in which dwell such distinguished guests as religion, art, etc. . . . I have already found a place for re-

[19] Binswanger's italics.

ligion, by putting it under the category of "the neurosis of mankind." But probably we are speaking at cross purposes, and our differences will be ironed out only after centuries. In cordial friendship, and with greetings to your charming wife, your Freud.[20]

Binswanger then adds in his book—and this is the central reason I quote the interchange—"As can be seen from the last sentence, Freud looked upon our differences as something to be surmounted by empirical investigation, not as something bearing upon the transcendental conceptions that underly all empirical research." [21]

In my judgment, Binswanger's point is irrefutable. We can gather empirical data, let us say on religion and art, from now until doomsday, and we shall never get any closer to understanding these activities if, to start with, our presuppositions shut out what the religious person is dedicated to and what the artist is trying to do. Deterministic presuppositions make it possible to understand everything about art except the creative act and the art itself; mechanistic naturalistic presuppositions may uncover many facts about religion; but, as in Freud's terms, religion will always turn out to be more or less a neurosis, and what the genuinely religious person is concerned with will never get into the picture at all.

The point I wish to make in this discussion is the necessity of analyzing the presuppositions one assumes and of making allowance for the sectors of reality—which may be large indeed—that one's particular approach necessarily leaves out. I vividly recall how, back in my graduate days in psychology some twenty years ago, Freud's theories tended to be dismissed as "unscientific" because they did not fit the methods then in vogue in

[20] Binswanger, *op. cit.*, p. 99.

[21] By "transcendental," Binswanger of course does not refer to anything ethereal or magical: he means the underlying presuppositions that point beyond the given fact, the presuppositions that determine the goals of one's activity.

graduate schools of psychology. I maintained at the time that this missed the point: Freud had uncovered realms of human experience of tremendous importance, and if they did not fit our methods, so much the worse for our methods; the problem was to devise new ones. In actual fact, the methods did catch up—perhaps, one should add, with a vengeance, until, as Rogers has stated, Freudianism is now the dogma of American clinical psychology. Remembering my own graduate-school days, I am therefore inclined to smile when someone says that the concepts of existential psychology are "unscientific" because they do not fit the particular methods *now* in vogue.

It is certainly clear that the Freudian mechanisms invite the separation into discrete cause-and-effect formulations which fit the deterministic methodology dominant in American psychology. But what also needs to be seen is that this making of Freudianism into the dogma of psychology has been accomplished at the price of omitting essential and vitally important aspects of Freud's thought. There is at present a three-cornered liaison, in tendency and to some extent in actuality, between Freudianism in psychoanalysis, behaviorism in psychology, and positivism in philosophy. An example of the first side of the liaison is the great similarity between Hull's drive-reduction theory of learning and Freud's concept of pleasure as the goal of behavior—both consist of the reduction of stimuli. An example of the second is the statement of the philosopher Herman Feigl, in his address at a recent annual convention of the American Psychological Association, that Freud's specific mechanisms could be formulated and used scientifically, but such concepts as the "death instinct" could not be.

But the trouble there is that such concepts as the "death instinct" were precisely what saved Freud from the full mechanistic implications of his system. These concepts always point beyond the deterministic limitations of his theory. They are, in the best sense of the word, a mythology. Freud was never content to let go of this mythological dimension to his thinking despite his great effort at the same time to formulate psychology in terms of his nineteenth-century biological presuppositions. In my judgment, his mythology is fundamental to the greatness of his contribution and essential to his central discoveries, such as "the unconscious." It was likewise essential to his radical contribution to the new image of man, namely, man as pushed by demonic, tragic, and destructive forces. I have elsewhere shown that Freud's tragic concept of the Oedipus is closer to the truth than our tendency to interpret the Oedipus complex in terms of discrete sexual and hostile relationships in the family.[22] The formulation of the "death instinct" as a biological *instinct* makes no sense, of course, and in this sense is rightly rejected by American behaviorism and positivism. But as a psychological statement of the tragic nature of man, the idea has great importance indeed and makes Freud's system point beyond any purely biological or mechanistic interpretation.

Methodology always suffers from a cultural lag. Our problem is to open our vision to more of human experience, to develop and free our methods so that they will as far as possible do justice to the richness and breadth of man's experience. This can be done only by analyzing the philosophical presuppositions. As Maslow pithily states in Chapter II of this book:

> It is extremely important for psychologists that the existentialists may supply psychology with the underlying philosophy which it now lacks. At any rate, the basic philosophical problems will surely be opened up for discussion again, and perhaps psychologists will stop relying on pseudosolutions or on unconscious unexamined philosophies they picked up as children.

[22] See "The Significance of Symbols," in *Symbols in Religion and Literature* (New York: Braziller, 1960).

A more perplexing and tricky question arises with respect to the problem of prediction in science. How much and to what extent does one insist that science be able to predict the behavior of the given individual? Pervin cites as one of the inadequacies of the existential approach the fact that in as much as it conceives of the individual as free and unique, it makes his behavior unlawful and unpredictable. But "predictable" is a highly ambiguous term. And "lawful" and "predictable" cannot be identified. What we find in psychotherapy is that the behavior of the *neurotic* personality can be predicted fairly rigidly, because his behavior is the product of compulsive patterns and drives. But although the healthy person is "predictable" in the sense that his behavior is integrated and he can be depended upon to act according to his own character, he always at the same time shows a *new* element in his behavior. His actions are fresh, spontaneous, interesting; and in this sense he is just the opposite of the neurotic and his predictability. This is the essence of creativity. Maslow again puts this well:

> Only the flexibly creative person can really manage future, only the one who can face novelty with confidence and without fear. I am convinced that much of what we now call psychology is the study of the tricks we use to avoid the anxiety of absolute novelty by making believe the future will be like the past.

I wish here only to indicate that we need to open up our view of science. This concern for a new breadth in not at all limited to those in the so-called existential wing of psychology. In his paper "Clinical Skills Revisited," Professor Richard Dana brings out a crucial point in the training of graduate students in psychology:

> I suspect that the common, salient outcome of our previous four or five (or six) graduate years was caution—not breadth or depth or scholarship or ability to generalize—but mere caution. A kind of trained adherence to limited infer-

ences from data collected under rigorous conditions of control. Caution is indeed necessary in diagnostic testing or
treating of other persons but caution alone is stifling and
blinding for either individuals or professions. . . . We pos-
sess the methodological sophistication; we lack the grand
concepts and may be diminishing our professional potential
for generation of theory by exclusive preoccupation with
science. To be sure, we must be scientists but we also must
be *sapient* humans, first.[23]

The existential psychological position is, in my judgment,
not at all antiscientific. But it does insist that it would be
ironic indeed if our very dedication to certain methodol-
ogies in psychology should itself blind us in our understanding of human beings. Helen Sargent was expressing
the mood of many of us when she proclaimed, in another
paper at an APA convention, "Science offers more leeway
than graduate students are permitted to realize."

Another topic on which the existential approach breaks
new ground is the *problem of the ego.* I say "problem"
advisedly. The ego has come into the center of psychoanalytic and psychological discussions lately; and although
the interest in it reflects a highly positive development, I
believe the term itself causes more problems than it solves.
It is especially important to discuss it here, albeit briefly,
because many psychologists assume that what existential
psychology is talking about is encompassed in psychoanalytic ego psychology. This is an error.

Freud originally described the ego as weak and passive,
pushed by the id on one side and the superego on the other;
a monarch not in command in his own house. Later he
gave to the ego the executive functions and specifically
described it as being the organizing center of the personality.[24] But he still saw the ego as essentially weak. I

[23] Paper given at American Psychological Association convention, September 1959.
[24] Sigmund Freud, *The Ego and the Id* (London: Hogarth
Press, Ltd., 1927).

think he was right on that point, for by virtue of its structural position in the ego–id–superego system, the ego must remain fundamentally without autonomy even in its own realm.

In the last few years, in response to contemporary man's great need for autonomy and a sense of identity, considerable interest has swung to "ego psychology" in the psychoanalytic movement. But what has resulted has been the handing over to the ego of the functions of autonomy, sense of identity, synthesis of experience, and other functions, more or less arbitrarily arrived at, which we suddenly discover the human being has to have. The result in the orthodox analytic movement is that many "egos" appear. Karl Menninger speaks of the "observing ego," the "regressive ego," the "reality ego," the "healthy ego," and so forth.[25] A Freudian colleague and friend of mine congratulated me after a speech in which I had attacked this concept of a horde of egos by remarking, with obvious irony, that I had a good "synthetic ego!" Some psychoanalysts now speak of "multiple egos in the same personality," referring not to neurotic personalities but to the so-called normal ones. To my mind "multiple egos" is a precise description of a *neurotic* personality.

The concept of the ego, with its capacity for being broken up into many discrete egos is tempting for experimental psychology, for it invites "the divide and conquer" method of study that we have inherited in our traditional dichotomized scientific method. But I am convinced that the concept of multiple egos has grave inadequacies, practically and theoretically. It is as though we suddenly voted our weak monarch many new powers; but the monarch becomes all the more frightened and nonplused because the throne on which he sits is in its very framework weak and unsound and his new powers only overwhelm him and confuse him the more.

[25] Karl Menninger, *The Theory of Psychoanalytic Therapy* (New York: Basic Books, 1958).

For in this picture of many different egos, where has the principle of organization vanished? If we have this multitude of egos, we have by definition lost the center of organization, the center of unity that any executive must have if he is to function as an executive. If it is countered that this picture of the multitude of egos reflects the fragmentation of contemporary man, I would rejoin that any concept of fragmentation presupposes some unity *of which* it is a fragmentation. Rapaport writes an essay entitled "The Autonomy of the Ego" as part of the recent development we are referring to; Jung has a chapter in one of his books entitled "The Autonomy of the Unconscious"; and someone could write an essay, following Cannon's "Wisdom of the Body," entitled "The Autonomy of the Body." Each would have a partial truth; but would not each be fundamentally wrong? For neither the ego, nor the unconscious, nor the body can be autonomous. Autonomy by its very nature can be located only in the *centered self*.

To be sure, the works on identity of Eric Erickson,[26] and that of Allen Wheelis,[27] go beyond the presuppositions of the orthodox sytem in psychoanalysis with respect to the ego and, therefore, are able to offer something of significance in this area. But the value of their work lies precisely at those points at which it does break the bounds of the previous system. And the ultimate limitations of their approach, as in the final chapter of Wheelis' *Quest for Identity*, seem to me to inhere in the impossibility of constructing a new basis within the traditional psychoanalytic framework.

I could conclude this point more comfortably if I had a nice solution to propose. But I do not. I can blame this situation partly on the limitations of our English language: the terms we must use, like "self" and "being,"

[26] Eric Erickson, *Childhood and Society* (New York: W. W. Norton, 1950).

[27] Allen Wheelis, *The Quest for Identity* (New York: W. W Norton, 1958).

are woefully inadequate. But whatever terms we us
must ask ourselves certain questions. At what poin
I experience the fact that *I am the one who has these
different egos*? What unity do I presuppose *of which* the
various egos are fragments? Such questions indicate that
logically as well as psychologically we must go behind the
ego–id–superego system and endeavor to understand the
"being" of whom these are different expressions. My self,
or my being (the two at this point are parallel), is to
be found at that center at which I know myself as the one
responding in these different ways, the center at which I
experience myself as the one behaving in the ways described
by these varied functions. The point I wish to make is
that *being* must be presupposed in discussions of ego and
identity and that the *centered self* [28] must be basic to such
discussions.

Other fruitful topics for study that the existential approach in psychology presents in a fresh light are *will
and decision;* the constructive functions of anxiety and
guilt; the concept and experience of *being-in-the-world*—a
concept which, though it has parallels to gestalt psychology
on the formal side, operates on a different level and has
exceedingly wide implications; the *significance of time,*
particularly future time, as indicated by Maslow in Chapter II.

7

I shall now cite as illustrations some of the newer forms
of psychotherapy developed in the general field of existential psychology.

On March 1, 1966, Mayor John V. Lindsay appointed
New York City's first Narcotics Coordinator. There were
two things that made this more interesting than the usual
routine appointment. One was that the young psychiatrist,

[28] These points are discussed more fully in Chapter IV.

Dr. Efren Ramirez, had already been known in the profession by rumor across the water from Puerto Rico, where he was director of the Addictions Research Center. He had been able to achieve, so the rumor had it, what almost no one else in the profession has been able to accomplish, namely psychotherapy with some hope of effective "cure" with that most difficult of all patients—the narcotics addict.

The second aspect of special interest was that Dr. Ramirez accomplished this on the basis of existential principles. *The New York Times* reported that he "blended existentialism into his psychiatry." After college, where he had been "fascinated by the existential views of Sartre and Camus and the possibilities of their application to psychiatry," he had gone on to medical training and internship at the Columbia Presbyterian Medical Center. Then serving as medical officer in the United States Air Force, he had begun to "hone his existentialist approach to psychiatry" in the treatment of addiction.

"I will tell an addict," *The New York Times* reporter quoted Dr. Ramirez, "I am a doctor. I'm not responsible for your being an addict. I can merely offer you the alternatives to take you out of the hole. The rest is up to you." [29]

Every new form of psychotherapy must stand up to the needs of a "new" type of patient, plus the frustrations and defeats experienced by the therapist. Dr. Ramirez writes:

> Fortunately, demonstrations of the inadequacies of my professional training during my formative years provided me with a challenge, rather than a deterrent, to embark, six years ago, on a serious attempt to explore the field of rehabilitation of character disorders and perhaps find some answers. My only other resource was a deep intellectual conviction that an existential attitude toward the problem was the best possible approach.[30]

[29] *The New York Times,* March 1, 1966.
[30] Efren Ramirez, "The Existential Approach to the Management of Character Disorders with Special Reference to Nar-

In his plan he divides the recovery process into three sections: induction, treatment, and reentry. In each stage, two existential principles play a central role, namely *encounter* and *responsibility*. The induction may begin on a street corner, or in a store-front office, and goes through the stages he calls "halfway in" and "detoxification." Dr. Ramirez stresses the importance of having exaddicts, that is cured addicts, make these induction encounters; for the cured addict is a walking proof that it is possible to "kick" the drug habit. In the process, he redefines various psychiatric concepts. "Help," for example, "means rather bringing the patient head on, through group or individual confrontations, with a lucid picture of his *own* make up; *interpersonal*, that is his relationships with fellow human beings and their institutions; and *impersonal* or that which is independent of human action—accident, death and other of nature's forces." [31] The concept of responsibility, which he terms the "basis of the existential approach," he defines as "the ability to confront reality directly and to respond to it in a positive manner . . . . To the extent that a person can accept responsibility for his life, he becomes a free moral agent." Ramirez notes that this view of the addict's responsibility for his own life is a "direct departure from the usual way in which sociopathic personalities have been handled in the past." [32] Dr. Ramircz, like many existentialist psychotherapists, does not make diagnosis and prognosis once treatment has begun, "for in our particular setting, they actually obstruct, or weaken the impact of the confrontation experience." [33]

The program for the control of drug addiction in New York has not been operating long enough to assess the results. But in Dr. Ramirez's program in Puerto Rico, of

cotic Drug Addiction," *Rev. of existen. Psychol. and Psych.*, p. 45.

[31] *Ibid.*, p. 50.

[32] *Ibid.*, p. 50–51.

[33] *Ibid.*, p. 50.

the hundred and twenty addicts who were part of the program, only seven have reverted to using drugs.

To illustrate the approach of Ronald Laing, who has been receiving increasing attention lately and whose thought is based on existential principles, I shall quote from his book, *The Politics of Experience*.[34] Arguing that psychotherapy does not need to become a pseudoesoteric cult, Laing writes:

> We must continue to struggle through our confusion, to insist on being human. . . . Existence is a flame which constantly melts and recasts our theories. . . . We hope to share the experience of a relationship, but the only beginning, or even end, may be to share the experience of its absence.[35]

"A revolution is currently going on in relation to sanity and madness, both inside and outside psychiatry," Laing writes as a kind of theme for this book. "The clinical point of view is giving way before a point of view that is both existential and social." We are, he believes, in the midst of a shift in approach no less radical than that three

[34] This section consists largely of sections of a review of the above book by Laing which I wrote for the *Saturday Review*, May 20, 1967.

[35] Laing demonstrates the existential approach also by his breadth: he represents a creative synthesis of a number of significant streams in the psychotherapeutic field. He is an associate member of the British Psychoanalytic Society and principal investigator of the Schizophrenia and Family Research Unit at the Tavistock Institute of Human Relations in London. Closely associated with American anthropologists like Gregory Bateson and Jules Henry, he is also concerned with contemporary sociology and has played a central role in the significant recent research on family therapy, reported in a previous book, *The Families of Schizophrenics*. And not least important, he is of that rare breed in which the scientist and artist dwell in the same skin: the last fifteen pages of this book consist of a long poem by Laing entitled "The Bird of Paradise."

centuries ago from the demonological to the clinical. When mental disturbances were classified as illnesses, a concerted endeavor was made to find in schizophrenic behavior certain symptoms and signs of a disease of unknown origin, presumed to be largely genetic-constitutionally determined. What actually happened, by and large, was that the patient was adjudged psychotic if he could not adjust to society's requirements.

We are now, Laing states, in the third stage, in which it is seen that schizophrenia is a strategy certain persons must choose in order to survive in an alienated world.

In over 100 cases where we studied the actual circumstances around the social event when one person comes to be regarded as schizophrenic, it seems to us that *without exception* the experience and behavior that gets labeled schizophrenic is *a special strategy that a person invents in order to live in an unlivable situation.*

What is refreshing and exciting in Laing is not his glorification of the irrational—of which he is sometimes accused by psychiatrists and psychologists who preach adaptation—but his frank challenge: "Adaptation to what? To society? To a mad world?" To Laing the height of irrationality is adjusting to what is called "normal"—to a world of Vietnam, a world in which cities not only poison their citizens physically through air pollution but shrink the individual's consciousness, a world in which "machines are already becoming better at communicating with each other than human beings with human beings. The situation is ironical. More and more concern about communication, less and less to communicate."

Laing's constructive contribution has been to blend the interpersonal theory of Harry Stack Sullivan with an existential, phenomenological foundation. These two go together, asserts Laing: the only way we can understand and deal with human beings is to clarify the "nature of being human"—which is ontology. "Any theory not founded on the nature of being human is a lie and a be-trayal of man." And such a theory will have, to the extent the therapist is consistent, inhuman consequences. He believes that a fundamental source of our confusion in psychology and psychiatry is the "failure to realize that there is an ontological discontinuity between human beings and it-beings." Here Laing is in accord with Martin Buber's theory that psychoanalysis always tends to transform the "I" into an "it."

Though Laing appreciates Freud more deeply than many who make a dogma of the master's teachings, he holds that we must frankly face the fact that Freud thought and wrote in an alienated age and to some extent is himself an expression of this alienation. "The metapsychology of Freud, Federn, Rapaport, Hartman, Kris, has no con-structs for any social system generated by more than one person at a time. . . . This theory has no category of 'you' . . . no concept of 'me' except as objectified as 'the ego.' " But it is precisely the function of psychotherapy to "remain an obstinate attempt of two people to recover the wholeness of being human through the relationship between them."

We need a form of psychology that does not dwell on be-havior to the exclusion of experience or experience without regard for behavior, but centers on the relation between experience and behavior.

Laing is aware of the widespread emphasis in our day, particularly in America, on studying the individual solely in terms of his behavior. Yet to the extent that we do so, we lose the person, for the human being is characterized by both inner experience and outer behavior; and the critical point is the relation between the two. Of this, comments Laing, "natural science knows nothing." A new method is required, one he calls social phenomenology:

> We are a generation of men so estranged from the inner world that many are arguing that it does not exist; and that even if it does exist, it does not matter. . . . Quantify the

heart's agony and ecstasy in a world in which when the inner world is first discovered, we are liable to find ourselves bereft and derelict. For without the inner the outer loses its meaning, and without the outer the inner loses its substance.

I have already implied that I do not agree with a main criticism of Laing—that he glorifies schizophrenia. Rather, he humanizes it. In this humanizing, Laing's words have in them the ring of Blake and Dostoevsky in literature, and of Sullivan in psychiatry.

Nevertheless there remains a real problem in Laing's work. If, with respect to psychic problems, he rejects the concept of "illness," what criteria, what norms does he have as alternatives? What structure does he propose that he, and the rest of us, build upon? His writings, which in this book have a somewhat fragmentary character, may well be misunderstood and misused as a justification for mere "feeling" or antiintellectualism. (The student can read that other books by Laing are not so open to this charge, particularly *The Divided Self*.)

Laing himself is no antiintellectual; he thinks with dedication and profundity. But the tension in consciousness of holding together such different streams of thought and science—the task that Laing essays—is great indeed. And consequently the tendency to slide into anarchy or go off on disintegrating tangents is also great. Laing has developed a framework in his ontological bases and has taken important steps toward a science of interpersonal relationship. We can hope he will continue to build on both.

Another form of existential psychotherapy to be mentioned is Victor Frankl's *logotherapy*. A Jew in Vienna when Hitler overran Austria, Frankl spent several years in a concentration camp. Out of this experience came a very good book, *From Death Camp to Existentialism*. He learned (as Bruno Bettleheim also did) that the concentration camp experience forces one to be an existentialist: when life is pared down to the sheer fact of existence and when nothing else has meaning there is still the basic freedom, namely the freedom to choose the attitude one takes toward one's fate. This may not change the fate, but it greatly changes the person.

Out of this experience Frankl developed logotherapy, a therapy that emphasizes man's search for meaning (logos). First, he bases logotherapy on the facts and presuppositions that increasingly people come to psychotherapists for help without presenting any symptom but with feelings of boredom, being "fed up," and lacking meaning in their lives. Secondly, psychiatry should deal with meanings—goals and ends of life. Thirdly, will and decision are an important ingredient of what Frankl calls logotherapy. Fourthly, specific symptoms are dealt with by means of "reciprocal intention." That is, there is anticipatory anxiety built up in the patient as he fights against doing the thing he is neurotically drawn to do (the symptom of his neurosis). This is reduced and a counteraction set in motion by telling him to "go ahead and smash the window." Though the patient does not, according to Frankl, go through with the act, what this "permission" really does is to remove the symptom as the preoccupation of the patient and bring into view the underlying problem. Here he finds the doctor is allied with him in the solution of this problem. The assets of this kind of therapy are obvious.

But the dangers are that logotherapy hovers close to authoritarianism. There seem to be clear solutions to all problems, which belies the complexity of actual life. It seems that if the patient cannot find his goal, Frankl supplies him with one. This would seem to take over the patient's responsibility and—if we accept Rogers' assumption —diminish the patient as a person.

I have selected some illustrations of the way existentialism has influenced three different men. I have omitted therapists like Leslie Farber and Helmut Kaiser, who are definitely within the existential tradition; Thomas Szasz and Bruno Bettleheim and a number of others whose work shows the impact of existential psychology, have been omitted for reasons of lack of space and my belief that their approach was already well known. The older representatives of the field, such as Binswanger, Straus, Minkowski, and Boss, are covered in the volume *Existence*. My own approach in psychotherapy is implicit in my two essays in this present book, as well as in *Existence*.

8

We shall now look at some of the criticisms of existential psychology. The first thing that becomes obvious is that many of these criticisms are based on misunderstandings, and some reveal the critic's outright anger at the existential approach. Some of these come from leaders in psychology and, therefore, must be considered.

Robert Holt, for our first example, in his general attack upon Allport's idiographic method, throws existential psychology into the same pot as Zen Buddhism. Both of these "fashionable doctrines suffer from the same fallacies." Holt holds that the "lure" of existential psychology is the "direct contact with the world, unmediated by concepts,"[36] in contrast to the "necessary distance imposed by the scientific necessity to abstract." He pronounces existential psychology as "mystical" and concludes that "mystical experience, like aesthetic experience, offers nothing to the scientist qua scientist except an interesting phenomenon that may be subjected to scientific study." [37] That is to say, it is not a form of psychology.

Now this is curious indeed. How can we rule out as not a form of psychology the theme of the Fourth Annual Conference on Psychotherapy in Barcelona in 1958, attended by the largest body in the world devoted to inquiry and

[36] This is a misunderstanding, as I have already pointed out.
[37] These quotations are from Robert Holt, "Individuality and Generalization in the Psychology of Personality," *Journal of Personality*, 30, 3 (September 1962).

discussion in the field of psychotherapy? And how can we so blandly rule out the most important development in psychology and psychiatry in Europe in the 1940s and 1950s? Can we blithely cast aside the great body of literature and research as shown by the bibliography of this book—Merleau-Ponty's work on perception, Erwin Straus' writings on the senses, Binswanger, Boss, Kuhn; to say nothing of books in this country such as Joseph Lyons' *The Psychology of Phenomena*, Bugenthal's *The Quest for Authenticity*, and so on and on? I shall distinguish below between Zen Buddhism and existential psychology. Here let me only point out that Holt himself exhibits the real obscurantism in science, namely to rule out certain subjects for study a priori. This is to contribute to the narrowness of science, which so many contemporary people are rightly attacking.

Likewise Sigmund Koch speaks of existential psychology as a "kind of escape from traditional restraints to an answer rather than to a problem. . . . " They [existential psychologists] do not seem to think like scientists . . . ." which means, in effect, not like Sigmund Koch. Why should they? It is becoming increasingly clear in our day that there is something radically wrong with setting science off as a special game with its own rules; this is a defensive science, and it is all to the good if some groups refuse to talk this esoteric language. And with respect to "retreating into answers," if Koch means not being preoccupied endlessly with tools and methodology but with substantive problems such as love and will and death, the existential psychologists will be glad to plead guilty to the accusation. There are many intelligent people who believe that the very trouble with psychology in our day is that we are so concerned with methodology and tools that we have largely removed science from being a help when we need it. Sigmund Koch reveals his own bias when he holds that Sartre's statement, "Existence precedes essence," is "not especially illuminating." [38] (I assume he does not mean factual information, which Sartre's statement is not supposed to give, but illumination in the sense of a principle of investigation.) But we have seen that Sartre's statement, whether one agrees with it or not, is very illuminating indeed. It is the extreme form of the statement of the principle that no logic or mathematics, no system or language, no morality or religion would have any cogency except that we human beings exist prior to the problem. Man, in his own existence, affirms these things. It is the ultimate statement of the concept "We *are* our choices" and of the responsibility which goes along with that. Though I only partially agree with this statement of Sartre's, I cannot avoid admitting that it is one of those seminal sentences that cast light over decades and centuries of research.

I shall now add my own view of some of the difficulties, criticisms, and problems that confront existential psychology. One valid criticism lies in the fact that the concepts in existential psychology lend themselves to being used in the service of *intellectualistic detachment*. Such terms as "ontological," "ontic," and even the term "existential" may be used to cover up a multitude of ways of relating (or not relating) that would seem to be most unexistential. The special seductiveness of the terms in this field is that they give a semblance of dealing with human reality when they may not be doing so at all. Obviously, we need first of all to confront our real experience, in psychotherapy and other forms of psychology, and then find the terms (which may not be the terms inherited from our European colleagues) that will most fully express and communicate this experience.

Another difficulty or danger in this approach, already

[38] This and preceding quotations are from Sigmund Koch, "Psychology and the Unitary Conceptions of Knowledge," in *Behavior and Phenomenology*, University of Chicago Press, 1964.

touched upon in our discussion of Laing, is the use of the existential approach in the service of *antiintellectualism*. It would be an ironic pity indeed if this approach were to be allied, covertly or overtly, with the antiintellectual tendencies that are now present in the country; certainly this was one of the abuses to which the existential movement in Europe fell unhappy heir. I do not refer here centrally to the beatnik or hippie movements in this country. Antirational, to be sure, the beatnik and hippie phenomena represent an endeavor to achieve a conviction of the subjective reality of the given moment of sense experience; and in this respect the movements have their understandable function, truncated and inadequate as they may be.

But the tendency to distrust reason as such in our culture has arisen from the fact that the alternatives presented to intelligent and sensitive people have seemed to be only arid rationalism on the one hand, in which one saved one's mind by losing one's soul, or vitalistic romanticism on the other, in which there has seemed at least a chance of saving one's soul for the time being. The existential approach is certainly opposed to the first; but to make a more difficult and subtle point, I am convinced it is opposed to the second as well. The existential approach in psychology as elsewhere is *not to be rationalistic or antirationalistic, but to seek the ground on which both reason and unreason are based*. This is what was sought by Kierkegaard, who was marvelously gifted logically and intellectually but preferred to be called a poet. This ground underlying both reason and unreason was what Nietzsche sought also and what he tried to reveal in his allegories and shafts of dazzling insight. We must not be "mis-ologists," Socrates cautioned. But the "lógos," the word that expresses and reveals reason, must be made flesh.

Another difficulty and danger already touched upon in the existential approach lies, in my judgment, in its identification in some quarters with Zen Buddhism. What I am to say here is not a criticism of Zen Buddhism as such; I respect it as a religious–philosophical attitude toward life. Some of its values are its emphasis on meditation, the value of silence, the eternal perspective and union of the self with nature. And I see its radical value for modern Western man as a corrective to the historical emphases to which our Western culture is heir—such as competition, over-emphasis on technology and material goods, and our overvaluation of work. All cultural developments are one sided: the psychology of the East is a corrective for the West and vice versa.

But if Zen Buddhism is to be taken on as a way of life itself by any Western individual, decades of religious discipline are obviously required. The danger in the identification of existential psychology with Zen Buddhism is the oversimplification of both. This oversimplification becomes a way of avoiding the difficult problems of anxiety and guilt to which we as Western men are heir. Indeed, whenever an attitude toward life, whether it be psychological, philosophical, aesthetic, or religious, is taken over from another culture, its adherents are invited to jump out of their own cultural skins; problems are oversimplified and by-passed because they are not present in the new attitude one takes over. C. G. Jung, who never could be accused of underestimating oriental thought, has firmly warned against the dishonesty inherent in this taking of religion from one culture to another without fully absorbing the foreign religion or culture.

Kierkegaard and, so far as I know, all the thinkers in the existential tradition down to Paul Tillich, insist that the problems of anxiety, guilt, ennui, and conflict of Western man cannot be avoided. Central in the existential tradition is the "either/or" emphasis, the insistence that only with a heightened awareness of these problems and decisions can problems be met. In my judgment, the existential approach is the achieving of individuality (including subjective individuality) not by by-passing or avoiding the conflictual realities of the world in which we immediately find ourselves—for us, the Western world—but by confronting these conflicts directly and, *through* the meeting of them, achieving one's individuality.

May I say in conclusion to this discursive but, I hope, helpful chapter that it will be clear that I have not tried to propose a new system or a set of dogma. The reader will note in the succeeding papers that not one of the contributors does this. Each says, in effect: "The existential development is, to my mind, important and significant; how does it cast light upon our present problems in psychology?" As the reader will have discovered for himself, my own attitude is one of doubt toward the tendencies to make existential psychology a new movement but of strong affirmation of the penetrating questions asked in this new approach. I strongly affirm also the insistence of the existential attitude that these questions be answered on the *human* level. I believe that there is in this approach the demand for, and the guiding principles toward, a psychology that will be relevant to man's distinguishing characteristics as man. It points, as Gordon Allport says in Chapter VI, toward a psychology of mankind.

II

Existential psychology— what's in it for us?

ABRAHAM H. MASLOW

I am not an existentialist, nor am I even a careful and thorough student of this movement. There is much in the existentialist writings that I find extremely difficult, or even impossible, to understand and that I have not made much effort to struggle with.

I must confess also that I have studied existentialism not so much for its own sake as in the spirit of, "What's in it for me as a psychologist?" trying all the time to translate it into terms I could use. Perhaps this is why I have found it to be not so much a totally new revelation as a stressing, confirming, sharpening, and rediscovering of trends already existing in American psychology (the various self psychologies, growth psychologies, self-actualization psychologies, organismic psychologies, certain neo-Freudian psychologies, the Jungian psychology, not to mention some of the psychoanalytic ego psychologists, the Gestalt therapists, and I don't know how many more).

For this and other reasons, reading the existentialists has been for me a very interesting, gratifying, and instructive experience. And I think this will also be true for many other psychologists, especially those who are interested in personality theory and in clinical psychology. It has enriched, enlarged, corrected, and strengthened my thinking about the human personality, even though it has not necessitated any fundamental reconstruction.

First of all, permit me to define existentialism in a personal way, in terms of "what's in it for me." To me it means essentially a radical stress on the concept of identity and the experience of identity as a *sine qua non* of human nature and of any philosophy or science of human nature. I choose this concept as *the* basic one partly because I understand it better than terms like essence, existence, and ontology and partly because I also feel that it can be worked with empirically, if not now, then soon.

But then a paradox results, for the Americans have *also* been impressed with the quest for identity (Allport, Rogers, Goldstein, Fromm, Wheelis, Erikson, Horney, May, *et al.*). And I must say that these writers are a lot clearer and a lot closer to raw fact, that is, more empirical than are, e.g., the Germans Heidegger and Jaspers.

(1) Conclusion number one is, then, that the Europeans and Americans are not so far apart as appears at first. We Americans have been "talking prose all the time and didn't know it." Partly, of course, this simultaneous development in different countries is itself an indication that the people who have independently been coming to the same conclusions are all responding to something real outside themselves.

(2) This something real is, I believe, the total collapse of all sources of values outside the individual. Many European existentialists are largely reacting to Nietzsche's conclu-

sion that God is dead and perhaps to the fact that Marx also is dead. The Americans have learned that political democracy and economic prosperity do not in themselves solve any of the basic value problems. There is no place else to turn but inward, to the self, as the locus of values. Paradoxically, even some of the religious existentialists will go along with this conclusion part of the way.

(3) It is extremely important for psychologists that the existentialists may supply psychology with the underlying philosophy that it now lacks. Logical positivism has been a failure, especially for clinical and personality psychologists. At any rate, the basic philosophical problems will surely be opened up for discussion again, and perhaps psychologists will stop relying on pseudosolutions or on unconscious, unexamined philosophies that they picked up as children.

(4) An alternative phrasing of the core (for us Americans) of European existentialism is that it deals radically with that human predicament presented by the gap between human aspirations and human limitations (between what the human being *is*, what he would *like* to be, and what he *could* be). This is not so far off from the identity problem as it might at first sound. A person is both actuality *and* potentiality.

That serious concern with this discrepancy could revolutionize psychology, there is no doubt in my mind. Various literatures already support such a conclusion, e.g., projective testing, self-actualization, the various peak experiences (in which this gap is bridged), the Jungian psychologies, various theological thinkers.

Not only this, but they raise also the problems and techniques of integration of this twofold nature of man, his lower and his higher, his creatureliness and his Godlikeness. On the whole, most philosophies and religions, Eastern as well as Western, have dichotomized them, teaching that the way to become "higher" is to renounce and

master "the lower." The existentialists however, teach that
both are simultaneously defining characteristics of human
nature. Neither can be repudiated; they can only be integrated. But we already know something of these integration techniques—of insight, of intellect in the broader
sense, of love, of creativeness, of humor and tragedy, of
play, of art. I suspect we will focus our studies on these
integrative techniques more than we have in the past.
Another consequence for my thinking of this stress on
the twofold nature of man is the realization that some
problems must remain eternally insoluble.

(5) From this flows naturally a concern with the ideal,
authentic, or perfect, or Godlike human being, a study of
human potentialities as *now* existing in a certain sense, as
current knowable reality. This, too, may sound merely
literary, but it is not. I remind you that this is just a
fancy way of asking the old, unanswered questions, "What
are the goals of therapy, of education, of bringing up
children?"

It also implies another truth and another problem that
calls urgently for attention. Practically every serious description of the "authentic person" extant implies that such
a person, by virtue of what he has become, assumes a new
relation to his society and, indeed, to society in general. He
not only transcends himself in various ways; he also transcends his culture. He resists enculturation. He becomes
more detached from his culture and from his society. He
becomes a little more a member of his species and a little
less a member of his local group. My feeling is that most
sociologists and anthropologists will take this hard. I
therefore confidently expect controversy in this area.

(6) From the European writers, we can and should
pick up their greater emphasis on what they call "philosophical anthropology," that is, the attempt to define
man, and the differences between man and any other
species, between man and objects, and between man and

robots. What are his unique and defining characteristics? What is as essential to man that without it he would no longer be defined as a man?

On the whole, this is a task from which American psychology has abdicated. The various behaviorisms do not generate any such definition, at least none that can be taken seriously. (What *would* an S-R man be like?) Freud's picture of man was clearly unsuitable, leaving out as it did his aspirations, his realizable hopes, his Godlike qualities. The fact that he supplied us with our most comprehensive systems of psychopathology and psychotherapy is beside the point, as the contemporary ego psychologists are finding out.

(7) The Europeans are stressing the self-making of the self, in a way that the Americans do not. Both the Freudians and the self-actualization and growth theorists in this country talk more about discovering the *self* (as if it were there waiting to be found) and of *uncovering* therapy (shovel away the top layers and you will see what has been always lying there, hidden). To say, however, that the self is a project and is *altogether* created by the continual choices of the person himself is almost surely an overstatement in view of what we know of, e.g., the constitutional and genetic determinants of personality. This clash of opinion is a problem that can be settled empirically.

(8) A problem we psychologists have been ducking is the problem of responsibility and, necessarily tied in with it, the concepts of courage and of will in the personality. Perhaps this is close to what the psychoanalysts are now calling "ego strength."

(9) American psychologists have listened to Allport's call for an idiographic psychology but have not done much about it. Not even the clinical psychologists have. We now have an added push from the phenomenologists and existentialists in this direction, one that will be *very* hard to

resist, indeed, I think, theoretically *impossible* to resist. If the study of the uniqueness of the individual does not fit into what we know of science, then so much the worse for the conception of science. It, too, will have to endure 1e-creation.

(10) Phenomenology has a history in American psychological thinking, but on the whole I think it has languished. The European phenomenologists, with their excruciatingly careful and laborious demonstrations, can reteach us that the best way of understanding another human being, or at least *a* way necessary for some purposes, is to get into *his* *Weltanschauung* and to be able to see *his* world through *his* eyes. Of course such a conclusion is rough on any positivistic philosophy of science.

(11) The existentialist stress on the ultimate aioneness of the individual is a useful reminder for us not only to work out further the concepts of decision, of responsibility, of choice, of self-creation, of autonomy, of identity itself. It also makes more problematic and more fascinating the mystery of communication between alonenesses via, e.g., intuition and empathy, love and altruism, identification with others, and homonomy in general. We take these for granted. It would be better if we regarded them as miracles to be explained.

(12) Another preoccupation of existentialist writers can be phrased very simply, I think. It is the dimension of seriousness and profundity of living (or perhaps the "tragic sense of life") contrasted with the shallow and superficial life, which is a kind of diminished living, a defense against the ultimate problems of life. This is not just a literary concept. It has real operational meaning, for instance, in psychotherapy. I (and others) have been increasingly impressed with the fact that tragedy can sometimes be therapeutic and that therapy often seems to work best when people are *driven* into it by pain. It is when the shallow life does not work that it is questioned and that there

occurs a call to fundamentals. Shallowness in psychology does not work either, as the existentialists are demonstrating very clearly.

(13) The existentialists, along with many other groups, are helping to teach us about the limits of verbal, analytic, conceptual rationality. They are part of the current call back to raw experience as prior to any concepts or abstractions. This amounts to what I believe to be a justified critique of the whole way of thinking of the Western world in the twentieth century, including orthodox positivistic science and philosophy, both of which badly need reexamination.

(14) Possibly most important of all the changes to be wrought by phenomenologists and existentialists is an overdue revolution in the theory of science. I should not say "wrought by," but rather "helped along by," because there are many other forces helping to destroy the official philosophy of science or "scientism." It is not only the Cartesian split between subject and object that needs to be overcome. There are other radical changes made necessary by the inclusion of the psyche and of raw experience in reality, and such a change will affect not only the science of psychology but all other sciences as well. For example, parsimony, simplicity, precision, orderliness, logic, elegance, definition are all of the realm of abstraction.

(15) I close with the stimulus that has most powerfully affected me in the existentialist literature, namely, the problem of future time in psychology. Not that this, like all the other problems or pushes I have mentioned up to this point, was totally unfamiliar to me, nor, I imagine, to *any* serious student of the theory of personality. The writings of Charlotte Buhler, of Gordon Allport, and of Kurt Goldstein should also have sensitized us to the necessity of grappling with and systematizing the dynamic role of the future in the presently existing personality, e.g., growth and becoming and possibility necessarily point toward the future, as do the concepts of potentiality and

hoping and of wishing and imagining; reduction to the concrete is a loss of future; threat and apprehension point to the future (no future = no neurosis); self-actualization is meaningless without reference to a currently active future; life can be a gestalt in time, etc., etc.

And yet the *basic and central* importance of this problem for the existentialists has something to teach us, e.g., Erwin Strauss's paper in *Existence* (17). I think it fair to say that no theory of psychology will ever be complete that does not centrally incorporate the concept that man has his future within him, dynamically active at this present moment. In this sense, the future can be treated as ahistorical in Kurt Lewin's sense. Also we must realize that *only* the future is *in principle* unknown and unknowable, which means that all habits, defenses, and coping mechanisms are doubtful and ambiguous because they are based on past experience. Only the flexibly creative person can really manage future, *only* the one who can face novelty with confidence and without fear. I am convinced that much of what we now call psychology is the study of the tricks we use to avoid the anxiety of absolute novelty by making believe the future will be like the past.

I have tried to say that every European stress has its American equivalent. I do not think that this has been clear enough. I have recommended to Rollo May a companion American volume to the one he has already turned out. And of course most of all this represents my hope that we are witnessing an expansion of psychology, not a new "ism" that could turn into an antipsychology or into an antiscience.

It is possible that existentialism will not only enrich psychology. It may also be an additional push toward the establishment of another *branch* of psychology, the psychology of the fully evolved and authentic self and its ways of being. Sutich has suggested calling this ontopsychology.

Certainly it seems more and more clear that what we call "normal" in psychology is really a psychopathology of the average, so undramatic and so widely spread that we do not even notice it ordinarily. The existentialist's study of the authentic person and of authentic living helps to throw this general phoniness, this living by illusions and by fear, into a harsh, clear light which reveals it clearly as sickness, even though widely shared.

I do not think we need take too seriously the European existentialists' harping on dread, on anguish, on despair, and the like, for which their only remedy seems to be to keep a stiff upper lip. This high-I.Q. whimpering on a cosmic scale occurs whenever an external source of values fails to work. They should have learned from the psychotherapists that the loss of illusions and the discovery of identity, though painful at first, can be ultimately exhilarating and strengthening.

III

Death—relevant variable in psychology

HERMAN FEIFEL

Even after looking hard into the imposing literature, both important and unimportant, which psychology encompasses, one is impressed by how slim and neglected is the systematized knowledge about attitudes toward death. This is surprising on a number of counts:

(1) Throughout man's history, the idea of death poses the eternal mystery which is the core of some of our most important religious and philosophical systems of thoughts, e.g., Christianity, wherein the meaning of life is consum-

* A portion of this paper is based upon work supported by a research grant, M-2920, from the National Institute of Mental Health, Public Health Service, and some of the material has already appeared in *The Meaning of Death*, ed. H. Feifel (New York: McGraw-Hill, 1959).

mated in its termination; existentialism and its striking pre-occupation with dread and death. This outlook has enormous practical consequences in all spheres of life, economic and political, as well as moral and religious.

(2) One of the more distinguishing characteristics of man, in contrast to other species, is his capacity to grasp the concept of a future—and inevitable death. In chemistry and physics, a "fact" is almost always determined by events that have preceded it; in human beings, present behavior is dependent not only on the past but even more potently, perhaps, by orientation toward future events. Indeed, what a person seeks to become may well, at times, decide to what he attends in his past. The past is an image that changes with our image of ourselves.

(3) Death is something that happens to each one of us. Even before its actual arrival, it is an absent presence. Some hold that fear of death is a universal reaction and that no one is free from it.* When we stop to consider the matter, the notion of the uniqueness and individuality of each one of us gathers full meaning only in realizing that we must die. And it is in this same encounter with death that each of us discovers his hunger for immortality.

(4) A little closer to the psychological hearth, Freud postulated the presence of an unconscious death wish in people, which he connected with certain tendencies toward self-destruction. Melanie Klein believes fear of death to be at the root of all persecutory ideas and so indirectly of all anxiety. Paul Tillich (33), the theologian, whose influence has made itself felt in American psychiatry, bases his theory of anxiety on the ontological statement that man is finite, subject to non-being. Insecurity may well be a symbol of death. Any loss may represent total loss. Jung sees the second half of life as being dominated by the individual's

* F. S. Caprio, "A study of some psychological reactions during prepubescence to the idea of death," *Psychiat. Quart.*, 1950, 24, 495-505; G. Zilboorg, "Fear of death," *Psychoanal. Quart.*, 1943, 12, 465-475.

attitudes toward death. In sum, there is growing recognition of the relationship between mental illness and one's philosophy of life and death.

Death themes and fantasies are prominent in psychopathology. Ideas about death are recurrent in some neurotic patients* and in the hallucinations of many psychotic individuals. There is the stupor of the catatonic patient, sometimes likened to a death state, and the delusions of immortality in certain schizophrenics. It has occurred to me that schizophrenic denial of reality may function, in certain cases, as a magical holding back, if not undoing, of the possibility of death. If living leads inevitably to death, then death can be fended off by not living. Also, a number of psychoanalysts† are of the opinion that one of the main reasons that shock measures produce positive effects in patients is that these treatments provide them with a kind of death-and-rebirth fantasy experience. It is relevant to note, nevertheless, that even when anxiety about death is discussed in the psychiatric literature, it is often interpreted essentially as a derivative or secondary phenomenon, frequently as a more easily endurable aspect of "castration fear" or as separation anxiety from or loss of the love object.‡

* W. Bromberg and P. Schilder, "The attitudes of psychoneurotics toward death," *Psychoanal. Rev.*, 1936, 23, 1-28; J. D. Teicher, " 'Combat fatigue' or death anxiety neurosis," *J. Nerv. Ment. Dis.*, 1953, 117, 234-243; A. Boisen, R. L. Jenkins, and M. Lorr, "Schizophrenic ideation as a striving toward the solution of conflict," *J. Clin. Psychol.*, 1954, 10, 388-391.

† E. g., O. Fenichel, *The psychoanalytic theory of neuroses* (New York: Norton, 1945); P. Schilder, "Notes on the psychology of metrazol treatment of schizophrenia," *J. Nerv. Ment. Dis.*, 1939, 89, 133-144; I. Silbermann, "The psychical experiences during the shocks in shock therapy," *Int. J. Psychoanal.*, 1940, 21, 179-200.

‡ C. W. Wahl, "The fear of death," *Bull. Menninger Clin.*, 1958, 22, 214-223.

(5) Further investigation of attitudes toward death can enrich and deepen our grasp of adaptive and maladaptive reactions to stress and of personality theory in general. The adaptation of the older person to the idea of death, for example, may well be a crucial aspect of the aging process; and study of attitudes toward death in the seriously ill and dying person, an experiment-in-nature, can provide us with fresh insights into the ways different individuals cope with severe threat.

In broader perspective, not only psychology but Western culture generally, in the presence of death, has tended to run, hide, and seek refuge in euphemistic language, in the development of an industry that has as a major interest the creation of greater "lifelike" qualities in the dead, and in actuarial statistics. The military makes death impersonal, and prevalent entertainment treats death not so much as tragedy but as dramatic illusion. Concern about death has been relegated to the tabooed territory heretofore occupied by diseases like tuberculosis and cancer and the topic of sex. With the weakening of Pauline beliefs concerning the sinfulness of the body and the certainty of an afterlife, there appears to be a concomitant decrease in the ability of people to contemplate or discuss natural death.*

Nevertheless, the assaults of two World Wars together with the heritage of a potential nuclear holocaust have tended in recent years to push life's temporality more into the foreground. The existentialist movement has been particularly conspicuous in rediscovering death as a philosophical theme and problem in the twentieth century. In a sense, the history of existential philosophy in its major phases is an exegesis of man's experience of death. The image of man that emerges is that of a time-bound creature.

The existentialism of our century as expressed in the

* E. N. Jackson, "Grief and religion," in Feifel, *op. cit.;* G. Gorer, "The pornography of death," *Encounter,* 1955, 5, 49-52.

philosophies of Simmel, Sheler, Jaspers, and Heidegger has placed the experience of death near the center of its analysis of the human condition. It has accented death as a constitutive part rather than the mere end of life, and highpointed the idea that only by integrating the concept of death into the self does an authentic and genuine existence become possible. The price for denying death is undefined anxiety, self-alienation. To completely understand himself, man must confront death, become aware of personal death.

Existentialism is certainly not a psychotherapeutic technique and makes no pretenses in that direction. I feel, however, that its orientation implies consequences of a psychotherapeutic kind, concerning which May will comment in greater detail in Chapter IV.

In the limited space available to me, I wish to indicate some general findings on attitudes toward death issuing from a continuing series of investigations I am now carrying on. They will have to be considered in the nature of an interim report, tentative and subject to change. I hope, nevertheless, that they will suggest therapeutic possibilities. The results are based on four major groups: 85 mentally ill patients with a mean age of 36 years; 40 older persons with a mean age of 67 years; 85 "normals" consisting of 50 young people with a mean age of 26 years, and 35 professional persons with a mean age of 40 years; and 20 terminally ill patients with a mean age of 42 years.

In response to the question "What does death mean to you?" two outlooks dominate. One views death in philosophic vein as the natural end process of life. The other is of a religious nature, perceiving death as the dissolution of bodily life and, in reality, the beginning of a new life. This finding, in a sense, broadly mirrors the interpretation of death in the history of Western thought. From these two opposing poles, two contrasting ethics may be derived. "On the one hand the attitude toward death is the stoic or skeptic acceptance of the inevitable, or even the repression

of the thought of death by life; on the other, the idealistic glorification of death is that which gives meaning to life, or is the precondition for the true life of man." *
This finding underlines the profound contradiction that exists in our thinking about the problem of death. Our tradition assumes that man is both terminated by death and yet capable of continuing in some other sense beyond death. Death is seen on the one hand as a "wall," the ultimate personal disaster, and suicide as the act of a sick mind; on the other, death is regarded as a "doorway," a point in time on the way to eternity.

The *degree* of mental disturbance per se in the patients, apparently, has little effect on their over-all attitudes toward death. Neither neurosis nor psychosis produces attitudes toward death that cannot also be found in normal subjects. The emotional disturbance seemingly serves to bring *specific* attitudes more clearly to the foreground. These results reinforce the findings of Bromberg and Schilder.† Incidentally, few normal people visualize themselves as dying by means of an accident. This is in contrast to the findings for the mentally ill patients, a good proportion of whom see themselves as dying by "crashing in a plane," "being run over by a tractor," "getting shot," etc.

When asked to express their preference as to the "manner, place, and time" of death, an overwhelming majority in all the groups want to die quickly with little suffering— "peacefully in your sleep," as most put it, or "having a coronary." The remainder want to have plenty of time in order to make farewells to family and friends. "At home" and "bed" are specifically mentioned by the majority as the preferred place of death. There are, naturally, personal idiosyncracies—"in a garden," "overlooking the ocean," "in a hammock on a spring day." About 15–20% in each group say it really does not make much difference

* H. Marcuse, "The ideology of death," in Feifel, *op. cit.*
† Bromberg and Schilder, *op. cit.*

to them where they die. One wonders whether these re-sponses do not reflect, on some level, a reaction to our modern way of dying. No longer do most of us receive death in the privacy of our homes with family about and attending, and with a minimum of medicine to prolong life. We die in the "big" hospital with its superior facilities for providing care and alleviating pain, but also with its im-personal intravenous tubes and oxygen tents. It is as if death's reality were being obscured by making it a public event, something that befalls everyone yet no one in particular.

With reference to the time of death, most people say they want to die at night because "it would mean less trouble for everyone concerned," "little fuss." The choice of night, outside of the contemplated peaceful end of life it connotes, has many engrossing symbolic overtones. Homer in the Iliad alludes to sleep (*hypnos*) and death (*thanatos*) as twin brothers, and many of our religious prayers entwine the ideas of sleep and death. Orthodox Jews, for example, on arising from sleep in the morning thank God for having restored them to life again.

While the data were being collected and evaluated, the implication suggested itself that certain persons who fear death strongly may resort to a religious outlook in order to cope with their fears concerning death. I thought it would be fruitful to get comparative data on religious and non-religious persons, particularly taking into account the "judgment" aspect after death as a possible important variable. The mean age of the religious group (N = 40) was 31.5 years; that of the nonreligious one (N = 42) was 34 years. The main beliefs that characterized the religious group, as distinguished from the nonreligious one, were credence in a divine purpose in the operations of the universe, in a life-after-death, and acceptance of the Bible as revealing God's truths. One should be cautious in considering the religious person as invariant; the same holds true for the nonreligious person. Individuals may derive values (sociability, emotional support, sense of belongingness, etc.) and need-satisfactions from religious membership and participation that are not necessarily related to religious belief and commitment. Also, individuals may frequently express a religious identification (tradition) without formal membership or commitment. And often, there may be a difference between the value-commitments of the individual and those required by the "official" theological structure of his particular faith.* In other words, some people may profess religious tenets but not practice them. Others may adopt religion as a kind of defense against "the slings and arrows of outrageous fortune." Then, there are those who incorporate their religious beliefs into everyday living activities. Sharper and more definitive categorization is needed in this field. For example, attitudes toward death may well vary among differing denominational groups. Our purpose, however, at this stage, was to get some general measure of fundamentalist or nonfundamentalist outlook.

The religious person, when compared to the nonreligious individual in our sample, is personally more afraid of death. The nonreligious individual fears death because "my family may not be provided for," "I want to accomplish certain things yet," "I enjoy life and want to continue on." The emphasis is on fear of discontinuance of life on earth—what is being left behind—rather than on what will happen after death. The stress for the religious person is twofold. Concern with afterlife matters—"I may go to hell," "I have sins to expiate yet"—as well as with cessation of present earthly experiences. The data indicate that even the belief in going to heaven is not a sufficient antidote for doing away with personal fear of death in some religious persons. This finding, together with the strong fear of death expressed in the older years by a substantial number of religiously inclined individuals, may reflect a

* D. J. Hager, "Religious conflict," *J. Soc. Issues*, 1956, 12, 3-11.

defensive use of religion by some of our subjects. In corresponding vein, the religious person in our studies holds a significantly more negative orientation toward the older years of life than does his nonreligious peer.

Along this line, I believe that the frenetic accent on, and continual search for, the "fountain of youth" in many segments of our society reflects, to a certain degree, anxieties concerning death. One of the reasons why we tend to reject the aged is that they remind us of death. Professional people, particularly physicians, who come in contact with chronic and terminally ill patients have noted parallel avoidant tendencies in themselves. Counterphobic attitudes toward death, for example, may be observed frequently among medical interns. Now this reaction on the part of the physician is understandable: the need to withdraw libido investment, relief from unmitigated tragedy, the reality that others may benefit more from his time, etc. But I would submit that some physicians often reject the dying patient because he reactivates or arouses their own fears about dying, that, in some, guilt feelings tied up with death wishes toward significant figures in their own lives play a role, not to speak of the wounded narcissism and lack of gratification of the physician whose function it is to save life being faced with a dying patient who represents a denial of his essential skills. I think it would prove interesting to pursue the relationship aspect of choice of occupation here, where the "saving of life" is paramount, with personal attitudes toward death in physicians. One of the unsuspected obstacles I have come up against in carrying on research in the area has been not the patient, but the physician. An hypothesis I hold, which is being continually reinforced, is that one of the major reasons certain physicians enter medicine is to master their own above-average anxieties about death.

We have been compelled, in unhealthy measure, to internalize our thoughts and feelings, fears and even hopes concerning death. One of the serious mistakes we commit, I think, in treating terminally ill patients is the erection of a psychological barrier between the living and dying. Some think and say that it is cruel and traumatic to talk to dying patients about death. Actually, my findings indicate that patients want very much to talk about their thoughts and feelings about death, but feel that we, the living, close off the avenues for their accomplishing this. A good number of them prefer honest and plain talk from physicians about the seriousness of their illness. They have a sense of being understood and helped rather than becoming frightened or panicking when they can talk about their feelings concerning death. There is truth in the idea that the unknown can be feared more than the most known, dreaded reality.

When the present investigation was initially broached, the question was raised, and rightfully so, as to the possible negative effect and "stress" aspects of the interview and testing procedures on the patients. In resulting fact, the vast majority of them showed no untoward reactions. Some of them actually thanked the project personnel for affording them the opportunity to discuss their feelings concerning death. There is almost nothing more crushing to a dying person than to feel that he has been abandoned or rejected. This realization not only removes support and prevents the patient's getting relief from the various kinds of guilt feelings that he has, but does not even permit him to make use of denial mechanisms that he may have been able to use up until then.*

Speaking of guilt, it is a startling fact that many hopelessly sick people feel guilty. This results from a number of reasons: (1) They often express the suspicion that their sickness and fate are self-inflicted and their own fault. (2) They assume, more or less, the role of the utterly dependent child. Some consciously apologize for the trouble and "fuss" they are causing. Our culture fosters a sense

* Hattie Rosenthal, "Psychotherapy for the dying," *Amer. J. Psychother.*, 1957, 11, 626-633.

of guilt in most of us when we are placed in the dependent role. (3) This is further extended in the dying person because of his feelings that he is forcing the living about him to face the necessity and finality of death, for which they will hate him. (4) Closely allied to this is the sick person's dim awareness of his envy of those who remain alive and of the wish, rarely entering consciousness, that the spouse, parent, child, or friend die in his stead. There is the thought that it may be this wish, in part, that breaks into action in those cases of seriously ill people who kill not only themselves but family and neighbors as well.*

The living respond with guilt of their own—for being alive and seeing someone else die, and, perhaps, for even wishing that the dying person hurry along on his way. In truth, most healthy people feel anxious and guilty at seeing someone else die. Being faced directly with the existential fact of death seems to cast a blight on ego functioning.

Yet, we are aware that human maturity brings along with it a recognition of limit, which is a notable advance in self-knowledge. In a certain sense, the willingness to die appears as a necessary condition of life. We are not altogether free in any deed as long as we are commanded by an inescapable will to live. In this context, the everyday risks of living, e.g., driving downtown, taking an airplane trip to Cincinnati, losing one's guard in sleep become almost forms of extravagant folly. Life is not genuinely our own until we can renounce it.† Montaigne has penetratingly remarked that "only the man who no longer fears death has ceased to be a slave."

Clinical observation prompts the reflection that for many individuals perception of death from a temporal distance and when it is personally near may be two quite different matters. Also, knowledge of the "external" degree of

* G. J. Aronson, "Treatment of the dying person," in Feifel, *op. cit.*

† W. E. Hocking, *The meaning of immortality in human experience* (New York: Harper, 1957).

threat alone appears to be an insufficient base on which to predict with any certainty how a person will react to it. Information that you are to die in the near future does not necessarily constitute an *extreme* stress situation for specific individuals. The person's character structure—the type of person he is—may sometimes be more important than the death-threat stimulus itself in determining reactions. In ongoing work, we hope to scrutinize closely the existing relationships here, i.e., relating attitudes toward death to the *kind* of person who has them.

My own tentative thesis is that types of reaction to impending death are a function of interweaving factors. I strongly support the outlook of Beigler* here. Some of the more significant ones tentatively appear to be: (1) the psychologic maturity of the individual; (2) kind of coping techniques available to him; (3) influence of such varying frames of reference as religious orientation, age, sex; (4) severity of the organic process; and (5) the attitudes of the physician and other significant persons in the patient's world.

The research in progress reinforces the thinking that death can mean different things to different people. Even in a rather narrowly defined cultural group, the non-homogeneous psychological quality of fear of death becomes evident.† Death is a multifaceted symbol whose specific meaning depends on the nature and fortunes of the individual's development and cultural context. "Death is terrible to Cicero, desirable to Cato, and indifferent to Socrates."

One *leitmotif*, however, that persists in coming to the fore when one works in the area is that the crisis is often not the fact of oncoming death per se, of man's unsur-

* J. Beigler, "Anxiety as an aid in the prognostication of impending death," *A.M.A. Arch. Neurol. Psychiat.*, 1957, 77, 171-177.

† G. Murphy, "Discussion," in Feifel, *op. cit.*

mountable finiteness, but rather the waste of limited years, the unassayed tasks, the locked opportunities, the talents withering in disuse, the avoidable evils that have been done. The tragedy which is underlined is that man dies prematurely and without dignity, that death has not become really "his own."

To conclude: A man's birth is an uncontrollable event in his life, but the manner of his departure from life bears a definite relation to his philosophy of life and death. We are mistaken in considering death a purely biologic event.* Life is not comprehended truly or lived fully unless the idea of death is grappled with honestly.

There is a pressing need for more reliable information and systematic, controlled study in the field. This is an area in which theoretical formulations have not been lagging behind an accumulating body of descriptive and empirical data. Research on the meaning of death and dying can enhance our understanding of the individual's behavior and yield an additional entryway to an analysis of cultures.

Let me not be misunderstood. I do not hold that the human condition is fully described by care and anxiety, dread and death. Joy, love, happiness provide clues just as valid to reality and being.† As Gardner Murphy‡ has discerningly pointed out, it is far from being established that *all* facing of death necessarily represents gains in mental health. In some studies of pilots during World War II,§ it was found that those who did not break down psychologically retained, in the moments of most extreme

---

* K. R. Eissler, *The psychiatrist and the dying patient* (New York: International Univ. Press, 1955).

† J. Taubes, "Mortality and anxiety." Unpublished paper, 1956.

‡ G. Murphy, *op. cit.*

§ R. R. Grinker and J. P. Spiegel, *Men under stress* (Philadelphia: Blakiston, 1945).

danger, the illusion of invulnerability. Apparently, there is a need to face death and also a need to face away from it.*

My point is that it is a much needed step forward for psychology to recognize that the concept of death represents a psychological and social fact of substantial import and that the dying words attributed to Goethe— "More light"—are particularly appropriate to the field under discussion.

* G. Murphy, *op. cit.*

IV

Existential bases of psychotherapy

ROLLO MAY

There are several endeavors in this country to systematize psychoanalytic and psychotherapeutic theory in terms of forces, dynamisms, and energies. The existential approach is the opposite of these attempts. We do not deny dynamisms and forces; that would be nonsense. But we hold that they have meaning only in the context of the existing, living being—if I may use a technical word, only in the *ontological* context.

If we are to have a science adequate to serve as a basis for psychotherapy, several guiding principles are required. First, *the science must be relevant to the distinguishing characteristics of what we are trying to understand, in this case the human being.* It must be relevant, that is, to the distinctive qualities and characteristics that constitute the human being as *human.* These are the characteristics that constitute the self as self, without which this being would not be what he is: a human being.

A second guiding principle is in opposition to the assumption in conventional science that we explain the more complex by the more simple. This is generally taken on the model of evolution: the organisms and activities higher on the evolutionary scale are explained by those lower. But this is only half the truth. It is just as true that when a new level of complexity emerges (such as self-consciousness in man), this level becomes decisive for our understanding of all previous levels. The principle here is, *the simpler can be understood and explained only in terms of the more complex*. This point is particularly important for psychology and is discussed more fully later in this chapter with the topic of self-consciousness.

A third guiding principle is this: our fundamental unit of study in psychotherapy is not a "problem" that the patient brings in, such as impotence; or a pattern, such as a neurotic pattern or sadomasochism or a diagnostic category of sickness, such as hysteria or phobia, ad infinitum; or a drive or pattern of drives. Our unit of study is, rather, *two-persons-existing-in-a-world, the world at the moment being represented by the consulting room of the therapist*. To be sure, the patient brings in all his problems, his "illness," his past history, and everything else simply because it is an integral part of him. But what is important is that the one datum that has reality at the time is that he creates a certain world in the consulting room, and it is in the context of this world that some understanding of him may emerge. This world and the understanding of it is something in which both persons, patient and therapist, participate. Our point here has far-reaching implications not only because it bears directly on our research and practice in psychotherapy, but also because it suggests the guiding lines of an existential approach to science.

Here is a patient, Mrs. Hutchens, who comes into my office for the first time, a suburban woman in her middle thirties. She tries to keep her expression poised and sophisticated. But no one could fail to see in her eyes something of the terror of a frightened deer or a lost child. I know, from what her neurological specialists have already told me, that her presenting problem is hysterical tenseness of the larynx, as a result of which she can talk only with a perpetual hoarseness. I have been given the hypothesis from her Rorschach that she has felt all her life, "If I say what I really feel, I'll be rejected; under these conditions it is better not to talk at all." During this first hour with her, I also get some hints of the genetic *why* of her problem as she tells me of her authoritarian relation with her mother and grandmother and of *how* she learned to guard firmly against telling any secrets at all. But if I am chiefly pondering these *why's* and *how's* of her problem, I will grasp everything except the most important fact of all, namely the living, existing person here in the room with me.

I propose, then, that we begin with the one real datum that we have in the therapeutic situation, namely, the existing person sitting in the consulting room with a therapist. Let us ask: What are the essential characteristics that constitute this patient as an existing person, that constitute this self as a self? I wish to propose six characteristics, which I shall call processes, that I find in my work as a psychotherapist. They can as well be called *ontological characteristics*. Though these are the product of a good deal of thought and experience with many cases, I shall illustrate them with episodes from the case of Mrs. Hutchens.

First, Mrs. Hutchens, like every existing person, *is centered in herself, and an attack on this center is an attack on her existence itself*. This is a characteristic that we human beings share with all living beings; it is self-evident in animals and plants. I never cease to marvel how, whenever we cut the top off a pine tree on our farm in New Hampshire, the tree sends up a new branch from heaven knows where to become a new center. But our principle has a particular relevance to human beings and gives a basis for the understanding of sickness and health, neurosis and mental health. Neurosis is not to be seen as a deviation from our particular theories of what a person should be. *Is not neurosis, rather, precisely the method the individual uses to preserve his own center, his own existence?* His symptoms are ways of shrinking the range of his world (so graphically shown in Mrs. Hutchens' inability to let herself talk) in order that the centeredness of his existence may be protected from threat, a way of blocking off aspects of the environment so that he may then be adequate to the remainder.

Mrs. Hutchens had gone to another therapist for half a dozen sessions a month before she came to me. He told her, in an apparently ill-advised effort to reassure her, that she was too proper, too controlled. She reacted with great upset and immediately broke off the treatment. Now, technically he was entirely correct; existentially he was entirely wrong. What he did not see, in my judgment, was this very properness, this overcontrol, far from being things that Mrs. Hutchens wanted to get over, were part of her desperate attempt to preserve what precarious center she had. As though she were saying, "If I opened up, if I communicated, I would lose what little space in life I have." We see here, incidentally, how inadequate is the definition of neurosis as a failure of adjustment. *An adjustment is exactly what neurosis is; and that is just its trouble.* It is a necessary adjustment by which centeredness can be preserved; a way of accepting *nonbeing,* if I may use this term, in order that some little *being* may be preserved. And in most cases it is a boon when this adjustment breaks down.

This is the only thing we can assume about Mrs. Hutchens, or about any patient, when she comes in: she, like all living beings, requires centeredness, and this has broken down. At a cost of considerable turmoil she has taken steps, that is, come for help. Our second process, thus, is: every existing person *has the character of self-affirmation, the need to preserve its centeredness.* The particular name we give this self-affirmation in human beings is "courage."

Paul Tillich's emphasis on the "courage to be" is very important, cogent, and fertile for psychotherapy at this point. He insists that in man, being is never given automatically, as it is in plants and animals, but depends upon the individual's courage; and without courage one loses being. This makes courage itself a necessary ontological corollary. By this token, I as a therapist place great importance upon expressions of the patients that have to do with willing, decisions, choice. I never let such little remarks the patient may make as "maybe I can," "perhaps I can try" slip by without my making sure he knows I have heard him. It is only a half truth to say that the will is the product of the wish; I emphasize rather the truth that the wish can never come out in its real power except with will.

Now as Mrs. Hutchens talks hoarsely, she looks at me with an expression of mingled fear and hope. Obviously a relation not only exists between us here but has already existed in anticipation in the waiting room and ever since she thought of coming. She is struggling with the possibility of participating with me. The third process is, thus: *all existing persons have the need and possibility of going out from their centeredness to participate in other beings.* This always involves risk; if the organism goes out too far, it loses its own centeredness, its identity—a phenomenon that can easily be seen in the biological world. If the neurotic is so afraid of loss of his own conflicted center that he refuses to go out and holds back in rigidity, living in narrowed reactions and shrunken world space, his growth and development are blocked. This is the pattern in neurotic repressions and inhibitions, the common neurotic forms in Freud's day. But it may well be in our day of conformity and the outer-directed man, that the most common neurotic pattern takes the opposite form, namely, the dispersing of one's self in participation and identification with others until one's own being is emptied.

At this point we see the rightful emphasis of Martin Buber in one sense and Harry Stack Sullivan in another, that the human being cannot be understood as a self if participation is omitted. Indeed, if we are successful in our search for these ontological processes of the existing person, it should be true that the omission of any one of the six would mean that we do not then have a human being.

Our fourth principle is: *the subjective side of centeredness is awareness.* Such awareness is present in forms of life other than human; it is certainly observable in animals. Howard Liddell has pointed out how the seal in its natural habitat lifts its head every ten seconds even during sleep to survey the horizon lest an Eskimo hunter with poised bow and arrow sneak up on it. This awareness of threats to being in animals Liddell calls *vigilance,* and he identifies it as the primitive, simple counterpart in animals of what in human beings becomes anxiety.

The first four characteristic processes are shared by the existing person with all living beings; they are biological levels in which human beings participate. The fifth process refers now to a distinctively human characteristic: self-consciousness. *The uniquely human form of awareness is self-consciousness.* Awareness and consciousness should not be identified. I associate awareness, as Liddell indicates, with vigilance. This is supported by the derivation of the term "aware," coming as it does from the Anglo-Saxon *gewaer, waer,* meaning knowledge of external dangers and threats. Its cognates are *beware* and *wary.* Awareness certainly is what is going on in an individual's neurotic reaction to threat, in, for example, Mrs. Hutchens' experience in her first hours that I am also a threat to her.

Consciousness, however, is not simply my awareness of threat from the world but *my capacity to know myself as the one being threatened, my experience of myself as the subject who has a world.* Consciousness, to use Kurt Goldstein's terms, is man's capacity to transcend the immediate concrete situation, to live in terms of the possible. It underlies the wide range of possibility that man has in relating to his world, and it constitutes the foundation of psy-

chological freedom. Thus, human freedom has its ontological base and I believe must be assumed in all psychotherapy.

In his book *The Phenomenon of Man,* the paleontologist
Pierre Teilhard de Chardin brilliantly describes how awareness is present, including the form of tropism, in all forms
of evolutionary life from amoeba to man. But in man a
new function arises, namely self-consciousness. Teilhard de
Chardin undertakes to demonstrate something that I have
always believed, that when a new function emerges, the
whole previous pattern of the organism changes. The total
gestalt shifts; thereafter the organism can be understood
only in terms of the new function. That is to say, it is only
a half truth to hold that the organism is to be understood
in terms of the simpler elements below it on the evolutionary scale. The other half of the truth is more crucial for
us, namely every new function forms a new complexity
that reorganizes all the simpler elements in this organism.
As I previously said, *the simple can be understood only in
terms of the more complex.*

This is what self-consciousness does in man. All the
simpler biological functions must now be understood in
terms of this new function. No one would, of course, deny
for a moment the old functions, or anything in biology
that man shares with less complex organisms. Take sexuality, for example, which we obviously share with all mam-
mals. Given self-consciousness, sex becomes a new gestalt,
as is demonstrated in therapy all the time. Sexual impulses
are then conditioned by the *person* of the partner; what
we think of the other male or female, in reality or fantasy
or even repressed fantasy, can never be ruled out. The fact
that the subjective person of the other to whom we relate
sexually makes least difference in *neurotic* sexuality, say
in patterns of compulsive sex or prostitution, only proves
our point the more firmly, for these situations require precisely the blocking off, the checking out, and the distorting
of self-consciousness. Thus, when we discuss sexuality in

terms of sexual objects, as Kinsey does, we may garner interesting and useful statistics; but we simply are not talking about human sexuality.

Nothing in what I am saying here should be taken as anti-biological in the slightest; on the contrary, I think it is only from this approach that we *can* understand human biology without distorting it. As Kierkegaard aptly put it, "The natural law is as valid as ever." I argue only against the uncritical acceptance of the assumption that the organism is to be understood only in terms of those elements below it on the evolutionary scale, an acceptance that has led us to overlook the self-evident truth that what makes a horse a horse are not the elements it shares with the dog but what constitutes distinctively, "horse." Now, *what we are dealing with in neurosis are those characteristics and functions that are distinctively human.* It is these that have gone awry in disturbed patients. The condition for these functions is self-consciousness—which accounts for what Freud rightly discovered, that the neurotic pattern is characterized by repression and blocking off of consciousness.

It is the task of the therapist, therefore, not only to help the patient become aware, but even more significantly, to help him *transmute this awareness into consciousness.* Awareness is his knowing that something is threatening from outside in his world—a condition that may, as in paranoids and their neurotic equivalents, be correlated with much acting-out behavior. But self-consciousness puts this awareness on a quite different level; it is the patient's seeing that *he is the one who is threatened,* that he is the being who stands in this world which threatens, that he is the subect who *has* a world. And this gives him the possibility of *in-sight,* of "inward sight," of seeing the world and his problems in relation to himself. And thus it gives him the possibility of doing something about his problems.

To come back to our too–long silent patient: After about twenty-five hours of therapy Mrs. Hutchens had the following dream. She was searching room by room for a baby in an unfinished house at an airport. She thought the baby belonged to someone else, but the other person might let her take it. Now it seemed that she had put the baby in a pocket of her robe (or her mother's robe), and she was seized with anxiety that it would be smothered. Much to her joy, she found that the baby was still alive. Then she had a strange thought, "Shall I kill it?"

The house was at the airport where she, at about the age of twenty, had learned to fly solo, a very important act of self-affirmation and independence from her parents. The baby was associated with her youngest son, whom she regularly identified with herself. Permit me to omit the ample associative evidence that convinced both her and me that the baby stood for herself, and specifically for consciousness of herself. The dream is an expression of the emergence and growth of self-consciousness, a consciousness that she is not yet sure is hers and a consciousness that she considers killing in the dream.

About six years before her therapy, Mrs. Hutchens had left the religious faith of her parents, to which, by way of them, she had had a very authoritarian relation. She had then joined a church of her own belief. But she had never dared tell her parents of this. Instead, when they came to visit, she attended their church in great tension lest one of her children let the secret out. After about thirty-five sessions, when she was considering writing her parents to tell them of this change of faith, she had, over a period of two weeks, spells of partially fainting in my office. She would become suddenly weak, her face would go white, she would feel empty and "like water inside" and would have to lie down for a few moments on the couch. In retrospect, she called these spells "grasping for oblivion."

She then wrote her parents informing them once and for all of her change in faith and assuring them it would do no good to try to dominate her. The following session, she asked in considerable anxiety whether I thought she would become psychotic. I responded that whereas anyone of us might at some time have such an episode, I saw no more reason why she should than any of the rest of us; and I asked whether her fear of becoming psychotic was not rather anxiety arising out of her standing against her parents, as though genuinely being herself, she felt to be tantamount to going crazy. (I have noted several times that patients experience this anxiety at being themselves as tantamount to psychosis.) This is not surprising, for consciousness of one's own desires and affirming them involves accepting one's originality and uniqueness. It implies that one must be prepared not only to be isolated from those parental figures upon whom one has been dependent but at that instant to stand alone in the entire psychic universe as well.

We see the profound conflicts of the emergence of self-consciousness in three vivid ways in Mrs. Hutchens, whose chief symptom, interestingly enough, was the denial of that uniquely human capacity based on consciousness, talking. These conflicts are shown in (1) the temptation to kill the baby; (2) the grasping at oblivion by fainting, as though she were saying, "If only I did not have to be conscious, I would escape this terrible problem of telling my parents"; and (3) the psychosis anxiety.

This brings us to the sixth and last characteristic of the existing person: *anxiety*. Anxiety is the state of the human being in the struggle against that which would destroy his being. It is, in Tillich's phrase, the state of a being in conflict with nonbeing, a conflict that Freud mythologically pictured in his powerful and important symbol of the death instinct. One wing of this struggle will always be against something outside the self. But even more portentous and significant for psychotherapy is the inner battle, which we saw in Mrs. Hutchens; namely, the conflict within the person as he confronts the choice of whether and how far he will stand against his own being, his own potentialities.

Thus, I take very seriously, if metaphorically, this temptation to kill the baby, or kill her own consciousness, as expressed in these forms by Mrs. Hutchens. I neither water it down by calling it "neurotic" and the product merely of sickness, nor do I slough over it by reassuring her, "Okay, but you don't need to do it." If I did these, I would be helping her adjust at the price of surrendering a portion of her existence, that is, her opportunity for fuller independence. The self-confrontation that is involved in the acceptance of self-consciousness is anything but simple: it involves, to identify some of the elements, accepting of the hatred of the past, her mother's hatred of her and hers of her mother; accepting her present motives of hatred and destruction; cutting through rationalizations and illusions about her behavior and motives, and the acceptance of the responsibility and aloneness that this implies; the giving up of childhood omnipotence, and acceptance of the fact that although she can never have absolute certainty about her choices, she must choose anyway.

But all these specific points, easy enough to understand in themselves, must be seen in the light of the fact that *consciousness itself implies always the possibility of turning against one's self, denying one's self*. The tragic nature of human existence inheres in the fact that consciousness itself involves the possibility and temptation at every instant to kill itself. Dostoevsky and our other existential forebears were not indulging in poetic hyperbole or expressing the after effects of too much vodka the night before when they wrote of the agonizing burden of freedom.

I trust that the fact that existential psychotherapy places emphasis on these tragic aspects of life does not at all give the impression that it is pessimistic. Quite the contrary. The confronting of genuine tragedy is a highly cathartic experience psychically, as Aristotle and others through history have reminded us. Tragedy is inseparably connected with man's dignity and grandeur and is the accompaniment, as illustrated in such dramas as Oedipus and Orestes, of the human being's moment of great insight.

In my judgment, the analysis of characteristics of the existing being—these ontological characteristics that I have tried to point out—can give us a structural base for our psychotherapy. It can also give us a base for a science of man that will not fragmentize and destroy man's humanity as it studies him.

V

Two divergent trends

CARL R. ROGERS

During the course of the convention at which these papers were initially read, I was called upon to comment on two presentations, one involving a general theory of psychotherapy based on learning theory, and the other the existential point of view in psychology and psychotherapy that now appears in the earlier chapters of this book. These two presentations symbolize in an interesting way two strong currents in present-day American psychology, currents that at the moment seem irreconcilable because we have not yet developed the larger frame of reference that would contain them both. Because my own interest is primarily in psychotherapy, I am going to limit myself here to a discussion of these trends as they appear in this field.

The "Objective" Trend

On the one hand our devotion to rigorous hard-headedness in psychology, to reductionist theories, to operational definitions, to experimental procedures leads us to understand psychotherapy in purely objective rather than subjective terms. Thus we can conceptualize therapy as being simply the operant conditioning of the client. The therapist reinforces, by appropriate simple measures, those statements expressing feelings, or those which report dream content, or those which express hostility, or those which show a positive self-concept. Impressive evidence has been produced indicating that such reinforcement does increase the type of expression reinforced. Hence the road to improvement in therapy, in this view, is to select more wisely the elements to reinforce, to have more clearly in mind the behaviors toward which we wish to shape our clients. The problem is not different in kind from Skinner's shaping of the behavior of his pigeons toward ping-pong playing.

Another variant of this general trend is what is known as the learning-theory approach to psychotherapy, which exists in several forms. Those S-R bonds are identified that are anxiety creating or that have caused difficulties in adjustment. These are labeled, and their origin and effects are interpreted and explained to the subject. Reconditioning or counterconditioning is then utilized so that the individual acquires a new, more healthy, and more socially useful response to the same stimulus that originally caused difficulty.

This whole trend has behind it the weight of current attitudes in American psychology. As I see them, these attitudes include such themes as: "Away from the philosophical and the vague. On toward the concrete, the operationally defined, the specific." "Away from anything which looks within. Our behaviors and our selves are nothing but objects molded and shaped by conditioning circumstances. The future is determined by the past." "Since no one is free, we had better manipulate the behavior of others in an intelligent fashion, for the general good." (How unfree individuals can choose what they wish to do, and choose to manipulate others, is never made clear.) "The way to do is to *do*, quite obviously." "The way to understand is from the outside."

The "Existential" Trend

Logical and natural. as this trend may be, suited as it is to the temper of our culture, it is not the only trend that is evident. In Europe, which has not become so involved in scientism, and increasingly in this country, other voices are saying: "This tunnel vision of behavior is *not* adequate to the whole range of *human* phenomena." One of these voices is Abraham Maslow. Another is Rollo May. Another is Gordon Allport. There are an increasing number of others. I would like, if I may, to place myself in this group. These psychologists insist, in a variety of ways, that they are concerned with the whole spectrum of human behavior and that *human* behavior is, in some significant ways, something more than the behavior of our laboratory animals.

To illustrate this in the realm of psychotherapy, I should like to cite, very briefly, some of my own experience. I started from a thoroughly objective point of view. Psychotherapeutic treatment involved the diagnosis and analysis of the client's difficulties, the cautious interpretation and explanation to the client of the causes of his difficulties, and a re-educative process focused by the clinician upon the specific causal elements. Gradually I observed that I was more effective if I could create a psychological climate in which the client could undertake these functions himself—exploring, analyzing, understanding, and trying new solutions to his problems. During more recent years, I have been forced to recognize that the most important ingredient in creating this climate is that I should be *real*. I have come to realize that only when I am able to be a transparently real person, and am so perceived by my client, can he discover what is real in him. Then my empathy and acceptance can be effective. When I fall short in therapy, it is when I am unable to be what I deeply am. The essence of therapy, as I see it carried on by myself and by others, is a meeting of two *persons* in which the therapist is openly and freely himself and evidences this perhaps most fully when he can freely and acceptantly enter into the world of the other. Thus, borrowing from some ancient phrases, I am inclined to say, "The way to do is to *be*." "The way to understand is from within."

The result of this kind of a relationship has been well described by May. The client finds himself confirmed (to use Buber's term) not only in what he is, but in his potentialities. He can affirm himself, fearfully to be sure, as a separate, unique person. He can become the architect of his own future through the functioning of his consciousness. What this means is that because he is more open to his experience, he can permit himself to live symbolically in terms of all the possibilities. He can acceptantly live out, in his thoughts and feelings, the creative urges within himself, the destructive tendencies he finds within, the challenge of growth, the challenge of death. He can face, in his consciousness, what it will mean to him to *be*, and what it will mean to not be. He becomes an autonomous human person, able to be what he is and to choose his course. This is the outcome of therapy, as seen by this second trend.

Two Modes of Science

We may well ask how these different trends in therapy could come about—the one symbolized by Dollard, Miller, Rotter, Wolpe, Bergman, and others, the second by May,

Ma..low, myself, and others. I believe the divergence arises in part out of a differential conception of and use of science. To put it in oversimplified fashion, the learning theorist says, "We know much about how animals learn. Therapy is learning. Therefore effective therapy will be composed of what we know about animal learning." This is a perfectly legitimate use of science, projecting known findings into new and unknown fields.

The second group approaches the problem differently. These individuals are interested in observing the underlying order in therapeutic events. They say, "Some efforts to be therapeutic, to bring about constructive change, are effective; others are not. We find that there are certain characteristics that differentiate the two classes. We find, for example, that in the helpful relationships, it is likely that the therapist functions as a real person, interacting with his real feelings. In the less helpful relationships, we frequently find that the therapist functions as an intelligent manipulator, rather than as his real self." Here too is a perfectly legitimate concept of science, the detecting of the order which is inherent in any given series of events. I submit that this second conception is more likely to discover the uniquely human aspects of therapy.

Empirical Method as a Rapprochement

I have tried to sketch briefly these two divergent currents, whose advocates often find communication difficult because their differences are so great. Perhaps one function I can serve is to indicate that scientific method itself provides a basis for rapprochement. Let me be more specific.

As May has stated his six principles, they must be abhorrent to many American psychologists because they sound so vague, so philosophical, so untestable. Yet I found no difficulty at all in deducing testable hypotheses from his principles. Here are some examples.

From his first principle: The more the *self* of the person is threatened, the more he will exhibit defensive neurotic behavior.

The more the self of the person is threatened the more his ways of being and behavior will become constricted.

From his principle number two: The more the self is free from threat, the more the individual will exhibit self-affirming behaviors.

From principle number three, the hypothesis is more complex, but still crudely testable: The more the individual experiences a climate free from threat to self, the more he will exhibit the need for, and the actualization of, participant behavior.

From principle number six: A specific anxiety will be resolved only if the client loses the fear of *being* the specific potentiality regarding which he has been anxious.

Perhaps I have said enough to suggest that our positivist tradition of operational definitions and empirical research may be helpful in investigating the truth of the ontological principles of therapy set forth by May, the principles of personality dynamics implicit in Maslow's remarks, and even the effects of different perceptions of death as set forth by Feifel. In the long run, it is likely, as Maslow hopes, that the involvement of psychological science in these subtle, subjective, and value-permeated fields will in itself bring about the next step in the theory of science.

An Example

To illustrate more clearly the way in which research may clarify some of these issues, let me leap into one of the most controversial differences, and illuminate it from some studies out of the past. One of the elements of existential thinking most shocking to conventional American psychologists is that it speaks as if man were free and responsible, as though choice constituted the core of his existence. This has been evident in our speakers today.

Feifel says, "Life is not genuinely our own until we can renounce it." Maslow points out that psychologists have been dodging the problem of responsibility and the place of courage in the personality. May speaks of "the agonizing burden of freedom" and the choice between being one's self or denying one's self. Certainly to many psychologists today these can never be issues with which the *science* of psychology can be concerned. They are simply speculations.

Yet bearing on precisely this point, I should like to bring in some research of a number of years ago. W. L. Kell, doing his graduate work under my supervision, chose to study the factors that would predict the behavior of adolescent delinquents.* He made careful objective ratings of the family climate, the educational experiences, the neighborhood and cultural influences, the social experiences, the health history, the hereditary background of each delinquent. These factors were rated as to their favorableness for normal development, on a continuum from elements destructive of the child's welfare and inimical to healthy development, to elements highly conducive to healthy development. Almost as an afterthought, a rating was also made of the degree of self-understanding, because it was felt that although this was not one of the primary conditioning factors, it might play some part in predicting future behavior. This was essentially a rating of the degree to which the individual was objective and realistic regarding himself and his situation, whether he was emotionally acceptant of the facts in himself and in his environment.

These ratings, on 75 delinquents, were compared with ratings of their behavior two to three years after the initial study. It was expected that the ratings on family climate and social experience with peers would be the best predictors of later behavior. To our amazement, the degree of self-understanding was much the best predictor, correlating

* C. R. Rogers, W. L. Kell, and H. McNeil, "The role of self-understanding in the prediction of behavior," *Jour. Consult. Psychol.*, 1948, *12*, 174-186.

.84 with later behavior, whereas quality of social experience correlated .55, and family climate .36. We simply were not prepared to believe these findings and laid the study on the shelf until it could be replicated. Later it was replicated on a new group of 76 cases, and all the essential findings were confirmed, though not quite so strikingly. Furthermore, the findings stood up even in detailed analysis. When we examined only the delinquents who came from the most unfavorable homes and who remained in those homes, it was still true that their future behavior was best predicted not by the unfavorable conditioning they were receiving in their home environment, but by the degree of realistic understanding of themselves and their environment that they possessed.

Here, it seems to me, is an empirical definition of what constitutes "freedom" in the sense in which Dr. May has used that term. As these delinquents were able to accept into consciousness all the facts regarding themselves and their situation, they were free to live out all the possibilities symbolically and to choose the most satisfying course of action. But those delinquents who were unable to accept reality into consciousness were compelled by the external circumstances of their lives to continue in a deviant course of behavior, unsatisfying in the long run. They were unfree. This study gives, I believe, some empirical meaning to Dr. May's statement that the "capacity for consciousness . . . constitutes the base of psychological freedom."

I have tried to point up the two diverging ways in which psychotherapy may be carried on. On the one hand, there is the strictly objective approach—nonhumanistic, impersonal, rationally based on knowledge of animal learning. On the other hand, there is the kind of approach suggested in the papers on this program, a humanistic, personal encounter in which the concern is with an "existing, becoming, emerging, experiencing being."

I have proposed that an empirical research method can

study the effectiveness of each of these approaches. I have tried to indicate that the subtlety and subjective qualities of the second approach are not a barrier to its objective investigation. And I am sure that it has been clear that in my judgment the warm, subjective, human encounter of two persons is more effective in facilitating change than is the most precise set of techniques growing out of learning theory or operant conditioning.

VI

Comment on earlier chapters

GORDON W. ALLPORT

Although each paper merits extended discussion, I shall be forced to limit myself to a brief comment on four issues that seem to be especially crucial:

Maslow asks: "What's in European existentialism for the American psychologist?" In a moment, I shall offer my own answer to this question—a paraphrase, I think, of Maslow's answer.

But, first, if we are candid, most of us will admit that we are repelled by much of the writing and theorizing of our European colleagues. Some of it seems to us turgid, verbalistic, and reckless. A few of the ideas are as bright and as illuminating as the dawn; but often these are then drowned in a sea of darkness. The early chapters of

Existence (17) were the dawn to me, later chapters sheer darkness.

The preceding chapters show very well how American psychology sets about recasting imported ideas, bringing order, clarity, and empirical testing to bear on them. American psychology has had few, if any, original theories of its own; but it has performed a great service in extending and rendering more precise the contributions of Pavlov, Binet, Freud, Rorschach, and others. Now I predict we can perform a like service for Heidegger, Jaspers, and Binswanger. The papers of this symposium have already taken sturdy strides in this direction. In particular, the comments by Rogers show how American psychology will seek to recast existential dogma into testable propositions.

On the positive side, Maslow finds several gains in existentialism. The movement causes us, for example, to give new weight to the concepts of identity, choice, responsibility, futurity; and it presses us toward improved methods of person perception, away from brittle, dream-book techniques and overintellectualization, and above all toward devices for the idiographic study of the unique individual. I would venture to sum up Maslow's points by saying: *Existentialism deepens the concepts that define the human condition.* In so doing, it prepares the way (for the first time) for a *psychology of mankind.* Let me explain what I mean.

A series of facts unites mankind—all mankind. The human being is born of a father and mother, ordinarily conceived and nurtured in love. He pursues certain biological goals; but he also pursues other goals which require him to establish his own identity, to take responsibility, to satisfy his curiosity concerning the meaning of life. He usually falls in love and procreates. He always dies alone. Along the way, he experiences anxiety, longing, pain, and pleasure.

This series of events is universal; but psychology has never before gone about its task with this sharpened perspective. For this reason our store of concepts and methods and our points of emphasis are defective in handling many items in this series. Existentialism invites us to fashion a universal psychology of mankind.

One of the neglected items is *death*, the subject of the excellent paper by Feifel. It strikes me as outrageous that he feels compelled to title it "Death—A Relevant Variable in Psychology." Of course it is a relevant variable. Why is it that at this late date we still need to be persuaded?

As Feifel points out, a person's philosophy of death is a large part of his philosophy of life. Some regard death as terrible, some as desirable, some as indifferent. Because individual variations are subtle and numerous, why have we up to now not included outlook on death in our studies of personality and in our therapeutic horizons? As Feifel also points out, Freud's dogma of the "death wish" has proved to be sterile. Far more promising are Feifel's own beginnings of empirical investigation. Instead of assuming, as Freud does, that all men "seek" death, we shall soon have a more discriminating and enlightening report on the matter.

I should like, however, to ask Feifel to study more closely the variable of religion. He reports tentatively that religious people in general seem to be more afraid of death. But he also properly hints that there are more ways than one of being religious. When he looks more closely into the relationship, I predict that he will find two opposite trends. People whose religious values are "intrinsic," that is to say, comprehensive and integrative in their lives (true ends-in-themselves), will be less afraid of death. By contrast, those with "extrinsic" religious values (defensive, escapist, ethnocentric) will be more afraid. My prediction here follows our discovery that ethnic prejudice is positively associated with an extrinsic type of religion, whereas the intrinsic type makes for tolerance and universalism of outlook.

The third issue is of a different kind. Both Maslow and Feifel find European existentialism too preoccupied with dread, anguish, despair, and "nausea," the only remedy for which is a stiff upper lip! The beatnik aspect of existentialism is European, not American, in flavor.

Trends in American existentialism will be (and are) far more optimistic. Sartre says there is "no exit." One is reminded of Epictetus the Stoic, who long ago wrote, "So your nose runs? What then, you fool, be glad you have a sleeve to wipe it on." Can anyone picture Carl Rogers offering such counsel?

American patients suffer as deeply and, as Maslow says, are as distressed by the shallowness of their lives as are European patients. Yet the emphasis on resignation, acceptance, even on the "courage to be" seems more European than American. Viktor Frankl, whose recent book, *From Death Camp to Existentialism*, strikes me as the wisest elementary book on the subject, holds out little hope beyond acceptance of responsibility and the discovery of a meaning in suffering. American movements of the quasi-existential order (client-centered, growth, self-actualization, and ego therapies) are more optimistic in their orientation.

Finally, what I consider to be the central theoretical issue is raised by May's stimulating Chapter IV. He seems to suggest that phenomenology (that is, taking the client's own view of himself as a unique being-in-the-world) is the first stage of therapy—and perhaps only the first stage. (I am reminded of Robert MacLeod's similar claim a few years ago, that phenomenology is a good starting point, but poor end point, for social psychology.)

Now May admits that true existentialists would go further. They would say that if we understand the *what* in its full reality and richness, the *why* will be included. But the case of Mrs. Hutchens, presented by Dr. May, does not follow this theoretical orientation. True, he depicts carefully her image of herself in a threatening world.

But his therapy relies heavily on psychoanalytic techniques. Her problem is conceptualized in the familiar Freudian manner involving the theory of reaction formation, displacement, sublimation, and projection. Mrs. Hutchens' unconscious is filled with Freudian, not existential, furniture.

The theoretical issue is this: May not the patient's distorted view of the world sometimes constitute his ultimate problem? May not the effective motives of the life lie wholly in the disordered outlook? (I have in mind a recently retired submarine commander who has an habitually domineering and impatient manner. He believes that others should obey him instantly and is accordingly sour and disordered in his perception of others. I doubt that his problem lies back in his childhood. Because of circumstances, he has evolved a distorted view of his social relationships—and *that* is his problem.)

In short, existentialists would no doubt claim that sometimes what we call "symptoms" are in fact the ultimate problem. More and more we are coming to ascribe motivational force to cognitive conditions (cf. Festinger's "cognitive dissonance" and Bartlett's "effort after meaning"). Instead of the patient's phenomenological view offering us only the first stage, perhaps it constitutes the whole problem; it is ultimate as well as preliminary for therapy.

Let me hasten to add that I do not claim that this condition always holds. Repressions may have to be cleared up; unconscious hostilities may have to be made conscious. Therapy may have to employ conventional depth techniques.

All that I am saying is that our symposium has raised what to me is the fundamental issue in motivational theory. May not (sometimes at least) an acquired world-outlook constitute the central motive of a life and, if it is disordered, the ultimate therapeutic problem? May not a person's philosophy of life, here and now, be a functionally autonomous motive? Need we always dig deeper than the presenting phenomenology?

My own view is that psychology urgently needs to make a distinction between lives in which the existential layer is, in effect, the whole of the personality, and other lives in which it is a mere mask for the rumblings of the unconscious.

Existential and phenomenological psychology: A selective bibliography

JOSEPH LYONS
(with the assistance of
Barbara May)

When an earlier edition of this bibliography was prepared, less than eight years ago, it was possible to include in 185 items a nearly exhaustive listing of "writings in English in which phenomenological or existentialist conceptions are applied explicitly to issues in the field of psychology." An attempt to do the same today would result, quite probably, in close to 1000 entries. Existentialism and phenomenology are no longer doctrines or even movements but, like modern psychoanalysis, influences that pervade every aspect of the current intellectual and artistic scene.

In order to keep the following bibliography down to manageable size, so as to fulfill its purpose of introducing students to the field, we have therefore had to be quite severely selective —and as a consequence a very large number of equally worthwhile items have been omitted. However, if we have covered the major figures and provided a means for beginning to read seriously in this area, our purpose will have been satisfied. For

those who would like to read more, in whatever direction their
interests lie, we would suggest that they turn to a number of
journals: *Review of Existential Psychology and Psychiatry,
Philosophy and Phenomenological Research, Philosophy Today,
Cross Currents, Journal of Humanistic Psychology, Journal of
Existential Psychiatry,* and *Journal of Existentialism.*

The bibliography is divided into three sections. The first contains fundamental works in this field as well as a selection of
the writings of the most important figures. The second section
comprises other works, and the third provides an introduction
to clinical and therapeutic issues. We have for convenience
grouped together the writings of each author plus other works
about him. Within each of the sections the listing is alphabetical
by major author; however, the full bibliography is numbered
sequentially.

Section I

1. Buber, M. *I and thou.* New York: Scribner, 1958.
   Poetic, mystic, and profound, this little book is the major
   contribution of a great philosopher of existentialist thought.
   Additional writings:
   2. The William Alanson White Memorial Lectures, 4th
      Series. *Psychiat.,* 20 (1957), 95–129.
   3. *Between man and man.* Boston: Beacon Press, 1955.
      "Fills out" and "applies" the theme of (1).
   4. *Knowledge of man,* M. Friedman (ed.). New York:
      Harper & Row, 1966.
5. Heidegger, M. *Being and time.* New York: Harper &
   Row, 1962.
   The fundamental (and very difficult) statement by one of
   the most important figures in modern philosophy; the work
   itself is the source for a major portion of contemporary
   existentialist thought and practice. Additional writings:
   6. *Existence and being.* Chicago: Regnery, 1949.
      Contains a long biographical and critical essay by
      Werner Brock and four essays by Heidegger.
   7. *What is philosophy?* New York: College and Uni-
      versity Press, 1964.
   8. Macquarrie, J. *An existentialist theology: A com-
      parison of Heidegger and Bultmann.* New York:
      Macmillan, 1955.
      A very lucid exposition, comparing Heidegger with
      the great Protestant theologian.

9. Arendt, H. *The human condition*. Chicago: University of Chicago Press, 1958.
   One of the best attempts to apply Heidegger's ideas to problems of history and social relations.
10. Husserl, E. "Phenomenology." In *Encycl. Brit.*, 17 (14th ed.), 1929, 699–702
    This is the only brief presentation, in English, of his own views, by the philosopher who founded the school of thought known as Phenomenology. Other selections from his voluminous writings, and important writings on his work, are:
    11. *Cartesian meditations*. The Hague: Nijhoff, 1960.
    12. *Phenomenology and the crisis of philosophy*. New York: Harper & Row, 1965.
        A number of his shorter works.
    13. Farber, M. (ed.). *Philosophical essays in memory of Husserl*. Cambridge, Mass.: Harvard University Press, 1940.
        See in particular the essays by Alfred Schuetz and by John Wild.
    14. ———. *The foundation of phenomenology: Edmund Husserl and the quest for a rigorous science of philosophy*. Cambridge, Mass.: Harvard University Press, 1943.
        The first seven chapters contain a full history of Husserl's early work.
    15. Ricoeur, P. *Husserl, an analysis of his phenomenology*. Evanston, Ill.: Northwestern University Press, 1967.
        A critical and sympathetic account by an important French philosopher.
    16. Thevenaz, P. *What is phenomenology? and other essays*. Chicago: Quadrangle, 1962.
        Perhaps the best brief account of Husserl's "system."
17. Jaspers, K. *Reason and existenz*. New York: Noonday Press, 1955.
    A basic work by a contemporary philosopher-psychiatrist whose thinking is closely allied to existentialism. Additional writings:
    18. "On my philosophy," in W. A. Kaufmann (ed.), *Existentialism from Dostoevsky to Sartre*. New York: Meridian, 1956.
        A good introduction to Jaspers as a person and to his views on science.

19. *General psychopathology* (7th ed.). Chicago: University of Chicago Press, 1963.
   The English translation of Jaspers' classic and very influential work in psychiatry.
20. *Nature of psychotherapy.* Chicago: University of Chicago Press, 1965.
21. Loewenberg, R. D. "Karl Jaspers on psychotherapy," *American Journal of Psychotherapy*, 5 (1951), 502–513.
22. Kierkegaard, S. *Concluding unscientific postscript.* Princeton, N.J.: Princeton University Press, 1941.
   One of the many contributions by the nineteenth century Danish thinker who, more than anyone else, may be called the first voice of modern existentialism. Other writings:
   23. *The concept of dread.* Princeton, N.J.: Princeton University Press, 1944.
   24. *Fear and trembling and Sickness unto death.* New York: Doubleday, 1954.
   25. *Either/Or.* 2 vols. New York: Peter, Smith, 1959.
   26. *Kierkegaard anthology.* New York: Modern Library, 1959.
27. Lacan, J. *The language of the self: The function of language in psychoanalysis.* Baltimore: Johns Hopkins Press, 1968.
   The only book thus far translated into English of the psychoanalyst who is considered by many as the most important figure in contemporary French thought. A complete bibliography of his writings may be found in the Appendix, pp. 263–268, of Yale French Studies, No. 36–37, 1966.
28. Marcel, G. *The existential background of human dignity.* Cambridge, Mass.: Harvard University Press, 1963.
   This work and the following (29) provide an introduction to the thought of a leading representative of Catholic existentialist thought.
   29. *Being and having: An existentialist diary.* New York: Harper & Row, 1965.
30. Maslow, A. *Religion, values and peak experiences.* Columbus: Ohio State University Press, 1964.
   A summary of the chief contributions of the psychologist who has been the major theoretician and inspiration for "Third Force" psychology, an American adaptation of existentialist thought. Other writings:

Bibliography 103

31. *The psychology of science: A reconnaissance.* New York: Harper & Row, 1966.

32. *Toward a psychology of being* (rev. ed.). Princeton, N.J.: Van Nostrand, 1968.

33. May, R., E. Angel, and H. F. Ellenberger (eds.). *Existence: A New Dimension in Psychiatry and Psychology.* New York: Basic Books, 1958.

This volume contains the first collection of significant contributions in this field and served to introduce an existential orientation to American readers. For a review, see:

34. Rogers, C. R. "To be is to do," Review of *Existence, Contemporary Psychology,* 4 (July 1959), 196–198.

35. Merleau-Ponty, M. *Phenomenology of perception.* New York: Humanities Press, 1962.

A basic work by the late French philosopher-psychologist, whose writings comprise the most important attempt to write a phenomenologically oriented psychological theory. Additional writings:

36. *The structure of behavior.* Boston: Beacon Press, 1963.

37. *Signs.* Evanston, Ill.: Northwestern University Press, 1964.

Merleau-Ponty's complete works, which range widely in the humanities, are being translated and published by Northwestern University Press. They include:

38. *Primacy of Perception.* Evanston, Ill.: Northwestern University Press, 1964.

39. *Sense and nonsense.* Evanston, Ill.: Northwestern University Press, 1964.

40. Ricoeur, P. *Fallible man.* Chicago: Regnery, 1965.

This and the following works are by an important contemporary French philosopher who is attempting a synthesis of existentialist, Marxist, and Protestant thought with the insights of psychoanalysis.

41. *Freedom and nature: The voluntary and the involuntary.* Evanston, Ill.: Northwestern University Press, 1966.

42. *Symbolism of evil.* New York: Harper & Row, 1967.

43. Rogers, C. R. *Counseling and psychotherapy.* Boston: Houghton Mifflin, 1942.

This work established the nondirective approach in psychotherapy. Rogers' thinking is first cousin to a phenomenological approach and has been of primary importance in regard to clinical issues, the philosophy of science, and the orientation of contemporary psychology. Additional writings:

44. "Person or science? A philosophical question." *Amer. Psychol.*, 10, 1955, 267–278.

45. *Client-centered therapy*. Boston: Houghton Mifflin, 1959.

46. *On becoming a person*. Boston: Houghton Mifflin, 1961.

47. —————— and Stevens, B. *Person to person*. Walnut Creek, Calif.: Real People, 1967.

48. —————— and Dymond, R. F. *Psychotherapy and personality change*. Chicago: University of Chicago Press, 1954.
    A report of a major research project on outpatient therapy.

49. *The therapeutic relationship and its impact: A study of psychotherapy with schizophrenics*. Madison: University of Wisconsin Press, 1967.

50. Sartre, J. P. *Being and nothingness*. New York: Philosophical Library, 1956.

The major work by Sartre, stating his position as a leading phenomenologist and existential philosopher. More than any other contemporary figure, he has spelled out his philosophy in a wide range of forms, including essays, literary criticism, novels, plays, and both philosophical and psychological works. His other writings, and important commentaries on them, include:

51. *Existential psychoanalysis*. Chicago: Regnery, 1953.
    An extract of relevant portions of his major work (50), with an introduction by Rollo May.

52. *Anti-semite and Jew*. New York: Schocken, 1948.
    A penetrating study that demonstrates the application of a phenomenological approach to social issues.

53. *The Emotions: Outline of a theory*. New York: Philosophical Library, 1948.

54. *The psychology of imagination*. New York: Philosophical Library, 1948.

55. *Nausea*. New York: New Directions, 1964.
    Perhaps the best expression in literary form of the existential approach to human problems.

56. *No exit and three other plays.* New York: Vintage, 1955.
    The flies may be read as an essay on memory and guilt, and *No exit* as a statement on the psychology of interpersonal relations.
57. *Literary Essays.* New York: Philosophical Library, 1957.
    An essay on the art of the film.
58. Grene, M. *Dreadful freedom: A critique of existentialism.* Chicago: University of Chicago Press, 1948.
    Reissued in 1959, by the same press, under the title of *Introduction to existentialism.*
59. Kuhn, H. *Encounter with nothingness: A study on existentialism.* Chicago: Regnery, 1949.
    One of the most authoritative of the commentaries on Sartre.
60. Stern, A. *Sartre: His philosophy and psychoanalysis.* New York: Liberal Arts Press, 1953.
61. Wyschogrod, M. "Sartre, freedom, and the unconscious." *Rev. Existent. Psychol. Psychiat.,* 1 (1961), 179–186.
62. Spiegelberg, H. *The phenomenological movement,* 2 vols. The Hague: Nijhoff, 1965.
    The definitive historical account of the origins and development of phenomenology.
63. Straus, E. W. *Psychologie der menschlichen Welt (Psychology of the human world).* Berlin: Springer, 1960.
    A collection of papers, some of them in English, by a distinguished philosopher-psychiatrist who is one of the founders of a phenomenological psychiatry and one of the most important of contemporary thinkers in this field. Additional writings:
64. The Fourth International Congress of Psychotherapy, Barcelona, Spain, September 1 through 7, 1958. *Psychosom. Med.,* 21 (1959), 158–164.
    Reviews the place of existentialist thought in the history of science.
65. *The primary world of senses.* New York: Free Press, 1963.
    A major theoretical contribution to a phenomenological, as contrasted with a behaviorist, psychology.
66. *Phenomenological psychology.* New York: Basic Books, 1966.
    A collection of his most significant papers, on top-

ics ranging from the dance and the upright posture to objectivity and freedom.

67. von Baeyer, W. and R. M. Griffith (eds.). *Conditio Humana.* New York: Springer, 1966.
   A collection of papers dedicated to Straus on his seventy-fifth birthday. Straus has also edited the volumes that report the proceedings of the first two Lexington Conferences on Phenomenology. They are:

68. *Phenomenology: Pure and applied.* Pittsburgh: Duquesne University Press, 1964.

69. ————, and Griffith, R. M. (eds.). *Phenomenology of will and action.* Pittsburgh: Duquesne University Press, 1965.

70. Tillich, P. *The courage to be.* New Haven, Conn.: Yale University Press, 1952.
   A basic work by the late theologian whose writings have been profoundly influential in setting an existentialist tone for contemporary religious thought. Additional writings:

71. "Being and love," *Pastoral Psychol.,* 5 (1954), 43–48.

72. "Psychoanalysis, existentialism, and theology," *Pastoral Psychol.,* 9, 1958, 9–17.

73. "Existentialism and psychotherapy," published simultaneously in *Existent. Inqu.,* 1 (1960), and *Pastoral Psychol.,* reprinted in Doniger, Simon, *The Nature of Man,* Harper & Row, 1962, pp. 42–55.

74. *"Love, power, and justice,"* New York: Oxford, 1960.

75. Colm, H. "Healing as participation: Comments Based on Paul Tillich's Existential philosophy," *Psychiat.,* 16 (1953), 99–111.

76. Leibrecht, W. *Religion and culture: Essays in honor of Paul Tillich.* New York: Harper & Row, 1959.
   Of particular interest are the contributions by Lowith, Takeuchi, Jaspers, and Marcel.

77. May, R. (ed.). *Symbolism in religion and literature.* New York: George Braziller, 1960.
   This collection contains an important paper by Tillich.

Section II

78. Allport, G. W. *Becoming: Basic considerations for a psychology of personality.* New Haven: Yale University Press, 1955.

A summary statement by an American psychologist who, like Maslow, served as inspiration for Third Force psychology in this country.

79. Barrett, W. *Irrational man: A study in existential philosophy*. New York: Doubleday, 1958.
A well-written commentary, one of the best introductions to the subject—particularly in regard to literary and historical aspects.

80. Berdyaev, N. A. *Freedom and spirit*. London: G. Bliss, 1935.
A well-known Russian philosopher who is in the "religious" existential tradition. See also:
    81. Nucho, F. *Berdyaev's philosophy: The existential paradox of freedom and necessity*. New York: Doubleday, 1966.

82. Bergson, H. L. *Time and free will, An essay on the immediate data of consciousness*. New York: Macmillan, 1913.
One of the important precursors of contemporary phenomenological thought in philosophy. See also:
    83. Minkowski, E. "Bergson's conceptions as applied to psycho-pathology," *J. Nerv. Ment. Dis.*, 63 (1926), 553–568.

84. Blackham, H. J. *Six existentialist thinkers*. New York: Macmillan, 1952.

85. Bugental, J. F. T. "Humanistic psychology: A new breakthrough," *Amer. Psycholog.*, 18 (1963), 563–567.
An introductory statement by one of the leaders in American Third Force psychology. Additional writings:
    86. *The search for authenticity*. New York: Holt, Rinehart and Winston, 1965.
    87. *Challenges of humanistic psychology*. New York: McGraw-Hill, 1967.
    An excellent collection of papers, edited by Bugental.

88. Buytendijk, F. J. J. "The phenomenological approach to the problem of feelings and emotions," in M. L. Reymert (ed.), *Feelings and emotions: The Mooseheart Symposium*. New York: McGraw-Hill, 1950.
One of the few papers in English by a leading Dutch phenomenologist; here he applies his approach to problems of physiology. Additional writings:
    89. "Experienced freedom and moral freedom in the child's consciousness," *Educ. Theory*, 3 (1953), 1–13.

90. "Philosophic basis of human relations," *Philosophy Today,* 2 (1958); 108–112.
91. "The function of the parts within the structure of the whole: The excitability of the nerves as a Phenomenon of life," *J. Indiv. Psychol.,* 15 (1959), 73–78.
92. *Pain: Its modes and functions.* Chicago: University of Chicago Press, 1962.

Buytendijk's writings on a wide variety of problems, including play, the role of women, and the mind of animals, have been translated into most European languages. A full bibliography of his work may be found in the appendix of the following book dedicated to him, which also contains interesting essays from a phenomenological viewpoint by Rutten, Duijker, van der Horst, and van Lennep:

93. Langeveld, M. J. (ed.). *Rencontre-Encounter-Begegnung* (Contributions to one human psychology, dedicated to Professor F. J. J. Buytendijk). Utrecht: Spectrum, 1958.
94. Camus, A. *The rebel: An essay on man in revolt.* New York: Knopf, 1957.
This essay, like his novels and other writings, is his expression in terms of art of his existentialist view of man.
95. Caruso, I. A. *Existential psychology.* New York: Herder and Herder, 1964.
96. Chotlos, J. W. and J. B. Deiter. "Motivation from a phenomenological viewpoint," *J. Existent. Psychiat.,* 2 (1962), 35–48.
97. Collins, J. D. *The existentialists: A critical study.* Chicago: Regnery, 1952.
Particularly good for its introduction to the thought of Kierkegaard.
98. Combs, A. W. and D. Snygg. *Individual behavior: A perceptual approach to behavior* (rev. ed.). New York: Harper, 1959.
This is a revision of an earlier work (1949) that first stated the position of the "American" school of phenomenological psychology. Additional writings:
99. Combs, A. W. "Phenomenological concepts in nondirective therapy," *Journal of Consulting Psychology,* 12 (1948), 197–208.
100. Combs, A. W. "A phenomenological approach to adjustment theory," *J. Abnorm. Soc. Psychol.,* 44 (1949), 29–39.
101. Snygg, D. "The need for a phenomenological sys-

tem of psychology," *Psycholog. Rev.*, 48 (1941), 404–424.

102. ———, and A. W. Combs. "The phenomenological approach and the problem of "unconscious" behavior: A reply to Dr. Smith," *J. Abnorm. Soc. Psychol.*, 45 (1950), 523–528.

103. Creegan, R. F. "A phenomenological critique of psychology," *Phil. Phenomenol. Res.*, 9 (1948), 309–315. See also:

104. "Remarks on the phenomenology of praise," *Phil. Phenomenol. Res.*, 6 (1945), 421–423.

105. "Phenomenology," in Harriman, P. L. (ed.), *Encycl. Psychol.* New York: Philosophical Library, 1946.

106. David, H. P., and H. von Bracken (eds.). *Perspectives in personality theory.* New York: Basic Books, 1957.
Based on the proceedings of an international conference; of particular interest are papers by Wellek, Nuttin, van Lennep, and one on femininity by Buytendijk.

107. De Beauvoir, S. *The second sex.* New York: Knopf, 1953.
A treatment of the "woman problem" by an associate and follower of Sartre.

108. Duncker, K. "On pleasure, emotion, and striving," *Phil. Phenomenol. Res.*, 1 (1940), 391–430.
This is a chapter, by a brilliant psychologist of the Gestalt school, from his unfinished book on motivation.

109. Feifel, H. (ed.). *The meaning of death.* New York: McGraw-Hill, 1959.
A collection of essays on an important "existentialist" theme.

110. Friedman, M. (ed.). *Worlds of existentialism.* New York: Random House, 1964.

111. Fromm, E. *Escape from freedom.* New York: Rinehart, 1941.
Fromm's humanist approach is closely allied to that of the existentialists, particularly in his writings about human relations. See also:

112. *Man for himself.* New York: Rinehart, 1947.

113. Gaffron, M. "Some new dimensions in the phenomenal analysis of visual experience," *J. Pers.*, 24 (1956), 285–307.
An excellent example of this method as applied to an experimental problem.

114. Gurwitsch, A. "The phenomenological and the psycho-

logical approach to consciousness," *Phil. Phenomenol. Res.,* 15 (1954), 303–319.

The viewpoint of one of the few philosophers who follows Husserl's thinking very closely. See also his recent book:

    115. *The field of consciousness.* Pittsburgh: Duquesne University Press, 1964.

116. Jonas, H. "The nobility of sight," *Phil. Phenomenol. Res.,* 14 (1953), 507–519.

One of the few papers in English on a central topic, the phenomenology of the senses and of sensory experience. See also:

    117. *The phenomenon of life.* New York: Harper & Row, 1966.

118. Katz, D. *The world of colour.* London: Kegan Paul, Trench, Trubner, 1935.

A classic work on the phenomenology of the experience of color.

119. Koyre, A. Influence of philosophical trends on the formulation of scientific theories. *Sci. Mon.,* 80 (1955), 107–111.

By the French translator of Heidegger's works.

120. Kuenzli, A. (ed.). *The phenomenological problem.* New York: Harper & Row, 1959.

An introductory source for papers by some leading American figures.

121. Laing, R. D. *The divided self: An existential study of sanity and madness.* Baltimore: Penguin Books, 1965.

By a leading British psychiatrist who has been influenced by existentialist thought and especially by Sartre. Additional writings:

    122. *The politics of experience.* New York: Pantheon, 1967.

    An important and quite original reevaluation of mental illness.

    123. ———, and A. Esterson. *Sanity, madness and the family.* New York: Basic Books, 1965.

124. Lauer, Q. "Four phenomenologies," *Thought,* 33 (1958), 183–204.

A discussion of Heidegger, Scheler, Merleau-Ponty, and Sartre, by a Jesuit phenomenologist and translator of Husserl. See also:

    125. *Phenomenology, Its genesis and prospect.* New York: Harper & Row, 1965.

126. Lynch, W. "The art of wishing vs. the willful act," *Rev. Existent. Psychol. Psychiat.*, 4 (1964), 213–224.
127. Lyons, J. "The psychology of angels," *Forum* 2 (1958), 28–30.
See also:
128. Magic, fate, and delusion. *Forum*, 3 (1959), 18–21.
129. *Psychology and the measure of man: A phenomenological approach.* New York: Free Press, 1963.
130. MacLeod, R. B. "The phenomenological approach to social psychology," *Psycholog. Rev.*, 54 (1947), 193–210. One of the very few papers on classical phenomenology in an American journal of psychology. See also:
131. "The place of phenomenological analysis in social psychological theory," in Rohrer, J. H. and M. Sherif (ed.), *Social psychology at the crossroads.* New York: Harper & Row, 1951.
132. May, R. *The meaning of anxiety.* New York: Ronald Press, 1950.
A review of the views of the major modern thinkers on this topic, written by a psychologist-psychoanalyst who has been one of the leading American figures in the spread of an existentialist influence. Additional writings:
133 *Man's search for himself.* New York: Norton, 1953.
134. The nature of creativity, in H. H. Anderson (ed.), *Creativity and its cultivation.* New York: Harper & Row, 1959.
135. "Intentionality, the heart of human will," *J. Humanist. Psychol.*, 5, 2 (Fall 1965), pp. 55–70.
136. *Psychology and the human dilemma.* Princeton, N.J.: Van Nostrand, 1967.
137. *Love and will.* New York: Norton, 1969.
138. McGill, V. J. "The bearing of phenomenology on psychology," *Phil. Phenomenol. Res.*, 7 (1947), 357–368.
A useful discussion of methodology.
139. Natanson, M. *Literature, philosophy and the social sciences.* The Hague: Nijhoff, 1962.
See also:
140. ——— (ed.). *Essays in phenomenology.* The Hague: Nijhoff, 1966.
141. Nuttin, J. "Consciousness, behavior, and personality," *Psycholog. Rev.*, 62 (1955), 349–355.
By a leading Belgian psychologist who combines modern

personality theory with influences from Husserl.

142. Pfander, A. *Phenomenology of willing and motivation.*
Evanston, Ill.: Northwestern University Press, 1967.
An important book by a follower of Husserl who is less
well known than he should be. For a discussion of his
views, see:

    143. Spiegelberg, H. "The idea of a phenomenological
    anthropology and Alexander Pfander's psychology
    of man," *Rev. Existent. Psychol. Psychiat.,* 5
    (1965), 80–105.

144. Royce, J. R. "Psychology, existentialism and religion," *J.
Gen. Psychol.,* 66 (1962), 3–16.
See also:

    145. *The Encapsulated man.* Princeton, N.J.: Van
    Nostrand, 1964.

146. Scheler, M. F. *The nature of sympathy.* London: Rout-
ledge and Kegan Paul, 1954.
Except for Sartre, Scheler has presented the only full-
scale treatise on love, sympathy, and the psychology of
emotion. He was a colleague, though never a disciple, of
Husserl, with a more pronounced "existential" tinge to
his thought. See also:

    147. *Man's place in nature.* New York: Farrar, Straus
    & Giroux, 1963.

148. Schuetz, A. "William James' conception of the stream of
thought phenomenologically interpreted," *Phil. and Phenomenol. Res.,* 1 (1941), 442–452.
Schuetz was one of the leaders in the application of phenomenological insights to problems of social action. See
also:

    149. "Common-sense and scientific interpretation of
    human action," *Phil. and Phenomenol. Res.,* 14
    (1953), 1–37.

150. Shinn, R. *Restless adventurers.* New York: Scribner's,
1968.

151. Sonneman, U. "The specialist as a psychological problem," *Soc. Res.,* 18 (1951), 9–31.
A brilliant paper on the "existential" problem of speciali-
zation. See also:

    152. "The human sciences and spontaneity: Outline of
    a revolution," *Amer. J. Psychoanal.,* 18 (1958),
    138–148.

153. Spiegelberg, H. "On the 'I and me' experience in childhood and adolescence," *Rev. Existent. Psychol. Psychiat.,*
4 (1964), 3–21.

154. Strasser, S. "Phenomenological trends in European psychology," *Phil. Phenomenol. Res.*, 18 (1956), 18–34.
An excellent review by a very competent scholar. For a book-length treatment, see:
    155. *Phenomenology and the human sciences: A contribution to a new scientific ideal.* Pittsburgh: Duquesne University Press, 1963.

156. Tiryakian, E. A. *Socialism and existentialism.* New York: Prentice-Hall, 1962.

157. Tolsma, F. J. "Some considerations on the phenomenon of aggression," *J. Ment. Sci.*, 99 (1953), 473–482.

158. Unamuno y Jugo, M. *Tragic sense of life.* New York: Dover, 1954.

159. Van Kaam, A. "Phenomenal analysis: Exemplified by a study of the experience of 'really feeling understood,'" *J. Indiv. Psychol.*, 15 (1959), 66–72.
See comments under 116. See also:
    160. "The impact of existential phenomenology on the psychological literature of Western Europe," *Rev. Existent. Psychol. Psychiat.*, 1 (1961), 62–91.
    161. *Existential foundations of psychology.* Pittsburgh: Duquesne University Press, 1966.

162. Von Hornbostel, E. M. "The unity of the senses," *Psyche,* 7 (1927), 83–89.
A fascinating essay, this is reprinted in Ellis, W. D. (ed.), *A source book of Gestalt psychology.* New York: Humanities Press, 1950.

163. Von Uexkuell, J. *Theoretical biology.* London: Kegan Paul, Trench, Trubner, 1926.
One of the earliest books in a related science to be influenced by Husserl. For more recent work, see the various writings of the zoologist Heini Hediger and the biologist Adolph Portmann.

164. Wann, T. W. (ed.). *Behaviorism and phenomenology: Contrasting bases for modern psychology.* Chicago: University of Chicago Press, 1964.
The papers delivered at a symposium at Rice University.

165. Wild, J. *Existence and the world of freedom.* New York: Prentice-Hall, 1963.
By one of the leading American phenomenological philosophers.

166. Winthrop, H. "The Verstehen claim in the behavioral sciences," *Rev. Existent. Psychol. Psychiat.*, 4 (1964), 141–157.

167. Wyschogrod, M. *Kierkegaard and Heidegger: The on-*

tology of existence. New York: Humanities Press, 1954. Difficult, but highly rewarding.

Section III

168. Allers, R. *Existentialism and psychiatry.* Springfield: Thomas, 1961.

169. Arbuckle, D. S. "Existentialism in counselling: The humanist view," *Pers. Guid. J.*, 43 (1965), 558–567.

170. Benda, C. E. "What is existential psychiatry?" *Amer. J. Psychiat.*, 123 (1966), 288–296.

171. Binswanger, L. "On the relationship between Husserl's phenomenology and psychological insight," *Phil. Phenomenol. Res.*, 2 (1941), 199–210.
   One of the foremost psychiatrists of Europe, Binswanger founded the discipline of existential analysis by transforming Heidegger's conceptions into therapeutic terms. See the translations of some of his cases in (33), and the following additional writings:

   172. "Existential analysis and psychotherapy," in F. Fromm-Reichman and J. L. Moreno (eds.), *Progress in psychotherapy, 1956.* New York: Grune and Stratton, 1956.

   173. *Sigmund Freud: Reminiscences of a friendship.* New York: Grune and Stratton, 1957.
      This report of a lifelong friendship is of importance for understanding the relations between existential analysis and psychoanalysis.

   174. Blauner, J. "Existential analysis: L. Binswanger's Daseinsanalyse," *Psychoanalytic Review*, 44 (1957), 51–64.

   175. Needleman, J. *Being-in-the-world, A study of Binswanger's psychology.* New York: Basic Books, 1963.
      The best source for an understanding of Binswanger's contributions, by an American philosopher and translator.

   176. Schmidl, F. "Sigmund Freud and Ludwig Binswanger," *Psychoanal. Quart.*, 28 (1959), 40–58.

   177. Weigert, E. "Existentialism and its relations to psychotherapy," *Psychiat.*, 12 (1949), 399–412.

178. Boss, M. *Meaning and content of sexual perversions. A daseinsanalytic approach to the psychopathology of the*

phenomenon of love. New York: Grune and Stratton, 1949.

Boss, a contemporary Swiss psychoanalyst, is a major interpreter of Heidegger's concepts in the therapeutic field. See also:

179. "Mechanistic and holistic thinking in modern medicine," *Amer. J. Psychoanal.*, 14 (1954), 48–54.
180. *The analysis of dreams.* New York: Philosophical Library, 1958.
    Built around an authorized and popularized statement of Heidegger's views, particularly in respect to his disagreement with Freud.
181. *Psychoanalysis and daseinsanalysis.* New York: Basic Books, 1963.

182. Braaten, L. J. "The main themes of existentialism from the viewpoint for psychotherapy," *Ment. Hyg.*, 45 (1961), 10–17.
183. Buhler, C. *Values in psychotherapy.* New York: Free Press, 1962.
    By one of the leaders in developing Third Force psychology.
184. Colm, H. "The therapeutic encounter," *Rev. Existent. Psychol. Psychiat.*, 5 (1965), 137–159.
185. Ellenberger, H. F. "Current trends in European psychotherapy," *Amer. J. Psychotherap.*, 7 (1953), 733–753.
    See also:
    186. "Phenomenology and existential analysis," *Canad. Psychiat. Assoc. J.*, 2 (1957), 137–146.
187. Farber, L. *The ways of the will: Essays toward a psychology and psychopathology of the will.* New York: Basic Books, 1966.
    By one of the most original of American psychiatrists.
188. Frankl, V. E. *The doctor and the soul: An introduction to logotherapy.* New York: Knopf, 1955.
    An Austrian psychiatrist, Frankl has founded a "system" of psychotherapy that is closely allied to existentialist thought. Additional writings:
    189. "On logotherapy and existential analysis," *Amer. J. Psychoanal.*, 18 (1958), 28–37.
    190. *From death camp to existentialism: A psychiatrist's path to a new therapy.* Boston: Beacon Press, 1959.
        Contains a moving account of his experiences in a concentration camp and the effect this had on his life and values.

191. *Psychotherapy and existentialism.* New York: Washington Square Press, 1967.
192. Polak, P. "Frankl's *Existential Analysis,*" *Amer. J. Psychotherap.,* 3 (1949), 617–622.
193. Weisskopf-Joelson, E. "Some comments on a Viennese school of psychiatry," *J. Abnor. Soc. Psychol.,* 51 (1955), 701–703.
194. Goldstein, K. *The organism: A holistic approach to biology derived from pathological data.* Boston: Beacon Press, 1963.
    First published in 1939, this is the major statement of a neurologist who was strongly influenced by Husserl. See also:
    195. *Human nature in the light of psychopathology.* New York: Schocken, 1963.
    196. "The smiling of the infant and the problem of understanding the 'other.' " *J. Psychol.,* 44 (1957), 175–191.
197. Hulbeck, C. R. "The existential mood in American psychiatry," *Amer. J. Psychoanal.,* 24 (1964), 82–88.
198. Kelman, H. et al. "Existentialism and psychiatry: A round-table discussion," *Amer. J. Psychoanal.,* 23 (1963), 20–38.
199. Lederman, E. K. "A review of the principles of Adlerian psychology," *Inter. J. Soc. Psychiat.,* 2 (1956), 172–184. Adler's approach has much in common with phenomenology. Additional writings:
    200. Neufeld, I. "The authentic life style: At the crossroads between existentialism and Individual Psychology," *Indiv. Psychol.,* 2 (1964), 9–23.
    201. Stern, A. "Existential psychoanalysis and Individual Psychology," *J. Indiv. Psychol.,* 14 (1958), 38–50.
    202. Van Dusen, W. "Adler and existence analysis," *J. Indiv. Psychol.,* 15 (1959), 100–111.
203. Lyons, J. "An interview with a mute catatonic," *J. Abnor. Soc. Psychol.,* 60 (1960), 271–277.
    See also:
    204. "Existential psychotherapy: Fact, hope, fiction," *J. Abnor. Soc. Psychol.,* 62 (1961), 242–249.
205. Moustakas, C. E. *Existentialist child therapy.* New York: Basic Books, 1966.
206. Schachtel, E. *Metamorphosis: On the development of affect, perception, attention, and memory.* New York: Basic Books, 1959.

By a psychologist who has been influenced by both psychoanalytic and phenomenological conceptions. For a more extended treatment, see:

207. *Experiential Foundations of Rorschach's Test*, New York: Basic Books, 1966.

208. Sonneman, U. "Existential analysis: An introduction to its theory and methods," *Cross Currents*, 3, 1955.

209. Tiebout, H. M., Jr., "Freud and existentialism," *J. Nerv. Ment. Dis.*, 126 (1958), 341–352.

210. Van den Berg, J. H. "The human body and the significance of human movement," *Phil. Phenomenol. Res.*, 13 (1952), 159–183.
   See also:
   211. *The phenomenological approach to psychiatry.* Springfield: Thomas, 1955.
      A useful introduction.
   212. "The handshake," *Philosophy Today*, 3/4 (1959), 28–34.

213. Van der Horst, L. "Mental health and religion," *Pastoral Psychol.*, 6 (1955), 15–21.
   See also:
   214. "The philosophical and psychiatric basis of psychosomatic medicine," *Acta Psychother., Psychosom., Orthopaedagog.*, 5 (1957), 1–9.

215. Van Dusen, W. "The theory and practice of existential analysis," *Amer. J. Psychotherapy*, 11 (1957), 310–322.
   See also:
   216. "Zen and Western psychotherapy," *Psychologia*, 1 (1958), 229–230.

217. Weisman, A. D. *The existential core of psychoanalysis: Reality sense and responsibility.* Boston: Little, Brown, 1965.

218. Wenkart, A. "Phenomenology and psychoanalysis," *Amer. J. Psychoanal.*, 24 (1964), 77–81.